Also by Marie Vassallo

Origins, 2014

Edition 1, 2025

YouTube channel

http://www.youtube.com/user/RiesKitchen

Blog

https://rieskitchen.blogspot.com.au/

First published by Rie's Kitchen 2025

Text copyright © Marie Vassallo 2025

Photographs copyright © Myles Abbott 2025

The moral right of the author has been asserted.

All rights reserved. Without limiting the rights under copyright reserved above, no part of this publication may be reproduced, stored in, or introduced into a retrieval system, or transmitted in any form or by any means (electronic, mechanical, photocopying, recording or otherwise), without the prior written permission of the copyright owner.

Design by Marie Vassallo and Myles Abbott

Photography by Myles Abbott

In my journey thus far, I have learned special tricks and gathered memorable stories. I owe a special thanks to Barcelona Cooking, MIMO Cooking School, my CWA of Victoria friends, and Lindsay Noss. Without their inspiration and the stories they've shared, the recipes in this book would be the lesser.

YouTube is a trademark of YouTube, LLC.

This book is dedicated to my friends and family, who share my love of food and life. There would be nothing on these pages without Myles Abbott — my friend, travel buddy and loving partner. His photographs, along with his filming and editing expertise, make my food come to life. His frank and fearless commentary on recipes in development brings out the best in each and every page.

Introduction

In 2013, I started compiling a cookbook to come to terms with the passing of my Dad, John Vassallo, who deeply influenced my cooking and eating. That book, Origins, expanded in 2015, featured some of my favourite recipes and preserving techniques—the foundation of Rie's Kitchen—and led to this second book, Journeys, which traces our culinary travels over the past 10 years. Recipes are grouped by region, each with a photo, so you can travel with me.

The first 'Rie's Kitchen' blog entry appeared in April 2008, launching a journey of growing, cooking, and demonstrating food. I've cooked at the Portarlington Mussel Festival, Royal Melbourne Show, CWA Christmas Fair and Masterclasses, Grampians Grape Escape, Prahran Market, Melbourne Food & Wine Festival, CAE, Box Hill TAFE, Farnham Street Community House, and Yarra Plenty Regional Libraries.

In 2014, I launched my YouTube channel, now with over 100 videos sharing our travels and skills. Feedback from viewers helped me explore new paths, improve recipe clarity, and try alternative ingredients.

I'm lucky to travel widely—taking cooking classes, visiting markets, and exploring vibrant food cultures. Myles and I often join guided market tours to better understand local traditions and produce. As someone with coeliac disease, these tours are especially helpful—I can ask questions in English to ensure I'm cooking safely back in our apartment. We especially loved the Kyoto market and La Boqueria in Barcelona. In France, no trip is planned without first checking local market days. Then, with a bag of regional specialties and fresh ingredients, the day begins.

Every recipe in this book is either gluten-free—like Hot Cross Buns—or includes simple tweaks, like with zucchini slice, to make them safe. Your non-gluten-free friends won't notice, and any coeliacs in your life will be grateful.

If you've been to one of my demonstrations, you'll know they're full of stories—Mum's 'knucklebone roster', Auntie Vivi's almond biscuits, Torquay spuds, pintxos in San Sebastián, food on a stick in Japan, tomato varieties in Europe... life revolves around food, family, and laughter. I hope you enjoy these stories and use the recipes to create your own.

Ciao,
Marie 'Rie' Vassallo

Contents

Family Table Treasures 7

European Quartet 41

New World Flavours 103

Spice and Silk 125

The Phoenician Table 151

Great Southern Land 189

Journeys Never Really End 249

Family Table Treasures

The concept of the family table is more than just a wooden structure surrounded by mismatched chairs, perhaps covered with a tablecloth (especially if guests were coming). It's the focal point of the house — a place where stories are shared, life lessons are passed down, and laughter and tears mix with the clatter of cutlery. It's where games are played, bills are scrutinised in tough times, and skirt hems are pinned. And, of course, it's where meals are shared.

I think we all learn valuable life lessons at the family table — cooperation, respect, empathy, and communication — all of which foster stronger family bonds and a sense of belonging. I didn't realise it at the time, but I also learned cultural acceptance and how food is one of the simplest yet most powerful expressions of love.

As I've gotten older, some of my strongest memories revolve around food: trying to feed my broad beans to the dog (she wouldn't eat them either!), the fight over whose turn it was for the knuckle bone from the roast leg of lamb (check the fridge for the roster!), and the hand being slapped away as someone tried to pinch a crunchy piece of pasta from the timpana before it was served. Food, love, sharing. Even when times were hard and there wasn't a lot to spare, the kitchen table was the happy place in our home.

In my twenties, as many of us left home, a group of friends would gather at my place for Sunday lunch or dinner. We took turns cooking the meal, and then it was shared. Some meals were fancy, some were basic — but what we ate didn't matter. What mattered was being together, laughing, crying, and supporting each other. The family we chose.

Through my volunteer work, it's become even clearer to me that food is the thread that brings people together. It shows each person they are valued, heard, and cared for. This chapter is dedicated to the recipes that evoke my strongest memories of togetherness.

Almond biscuits (Nonna biscuits)

Makes 30

Almond biscuits (Biskuttini tal-Lewz Morr) are a traditional Maltese treat often enjoyed with coffee. To me, these biscuits symbolize family. My Aunt Vicky would always have a box of her homemade biscuits ready for whenever we visited. They were consistently adorned with almonds. She took great delight in the fact that, among all the traditional Maltese dishes offered at family gatherings, I always made a beeline for her biscuits. They are gluten-free and, quite frankly, delicious. My Aunt Mary also made these biscuits — her version always included lemon zest and was decorated with glacé cherries.

I've incorporated elements from both of my aunts' recipes, and so I have named these "nonna biscuits" in honor of these two incredible cooks.

- 400 g almond meal
- 375 g caster sugar
- 4 egg whites
- 1 tsp almond essence
- Zest of 1 lemon
- 30 whole blanched almonds

Preheat oven to 180°C fan/200°C.

Lightly beat egg whites with a fork. In a large bowl mix together all ingredients until the sugar dissolves. The mixture will be sticky.

Roll teaspoonful of mixture into small balls and place on a tray lined with baking paper, about 3 cm apart. Place an almond on top of each ball.

Bake for 15-20 minutes. Allow to cool on the tray before placing on a cooling rack.

Store in an airtight container.

https://youtu.be/up1lTbhu55o

Gluten free chocolate self saucing puddings

Serves 6

Who doesn't love chocolate? With winter starting to creep in, it's time to start firing up those warming winter desserts. This recipe is perfect for a family dinner, and equally suitable to serve to dinner guests. The cake is light and fluffy, and the rich luscious gooey sauce hidden under the cake brings smiles to all diners' faces. Most of my guests don't even know that they are eating gluten-free with this recipe, and it has become an extended family favourite. I like to serve with a dollop of thick cream or a scoop of good vanilla ice cream.

- 85 g white rice flour
- 3 tbl corn flour
- 3 tbl soy flour
- 1 tsp bicarbonate of soda
- 2 tsp baking powder
- 140 g caster sugar
- ½ cup cocoa powder
- ¾ cup milk
- 2 regular-sized eggs, lightly beaten
- 40 g butter, melted
- 1 tsp vanilla extract

Sauce:
- 140 g brown sugar
- 2 tbl cocoa powder
- 1¾ cups hot water

Preheat oven to 180°C fan/200°C.

Sift together flours, bicarbonate, baking powder, caster sugar and cocoa in a large bowl.

Whisk these ingredients to ensure they are well mixed.

In a separate bowl, mix together eggs, butter, milk and vanilla.

Add to dry ingredients, then mix until well combined.

Ladle into 6 greased ramekins, no more than ¾ filled (Do not add too much, if needed use 7 ramekins).

Then to make the sauce combine brown sugar and additional cocoa.

Spoon evenly on to the ramekins.

Across the back of a spoon, pour ¼ cup of hot water into each ramekin, so as to get the water to float on the top, not disturbing the brown sugar mixture.

Place the ramekins on a tray, and then into the oven for 25 mins.

https://youtu.be/XZ1hXnu9ZYc

Christmas cake

Serves 10+

In the Anglo tradition, Christmas cakes are fruit cakes, often decorated with layers of almond icing, a thick coat of royal icing, and then topped off with decorations. There is a myriad of fruit cake variations: boiled fruit cakes, light fruit cakes, nut-free cakes, some with alcohol, some alcohol-free, and heavy fruit cakes – and that only covers the traditional Anglo fruit cake! Let's demystify the process of making a fruit cake, step by step.

History

The first recorded fruit cakes were baked by the Egyptians. These cakes, based on barley flour and incorporating fruit and nuts, were placed in tombs to aid the souls in the afterlife. The Romans enhanced this recipe with pine nuts, pomegranate seeds, anise, cumin, and honeyed wine, creating a cake known as "Satura," which was given to soldiers before battle. From the 18th century onwards, the consumption of fruit and cakes coincided with the winter solstice and the nut harvest, leading to a greater emphasis on nuts in the recipe. Older recipes predominantly featured figs and dates, but in more contemporary versions, coloured glacé cherries (for that Christmas colour), pineapple, apricots, and other dried fruits are used. Today, spices typically include cinnamon, ginger, vanilla, and citrus peel.

Aging

Alcohol is often incorporated to prolong the cake's longevity, which can be achieved in four ways:

1. Soaking the fruit in rum or brandy for at least 48 hours, reserving any leftover soaking liquid to use in either step 2 or 3 below.

2. Perforating the bottom of the cake or brushing it with alcohol every 1-2 weeks.

3. Wrapping the cake in an alcohol-soaked cheesecloth and storing it in an airtight container. You will also need to perform step 2 regularly.

4. Employing a combination of all three methods listed above!

Dark vs Light

Dark cakes are made with molasses, brown sugar, dark fruits like currants and raisins, and dark spirits. They generally have a long shelf life.

Light cakes, which have a shorter shelf life, are made with granulated sugar, coloured fruit, and often without alcohol.

Boiled

This is a somewhat misleading term. The cake isn't boiled; it's baked in the oven like its light and dark counterparts. The distinguishing factor is that the fruit, sugar, and butter are boiled with some water for about 10 minutes to plump and soften the fruit before being combined with the flour and other ingredients.

In my family, we always purchased a charity Christmas Fruit Cake from the Lions Club. These cakes were always eaten by the adults, while we kids definitely preferred sweeter treats. It wasn't until last year, when I was making some Christmas cakes for the Country Women's Association of Victoria Christmas Fare, that Myles asked why I never made us a Christmas cake. Good question! Amid all the other Christmas baking, I never really found the time to make one for us. Myles' dad, Ivan, loved fruit cake, and they evoke a strong sense of nostalgia for Myles. So this year, in addition to the ones I've baked for the Fair, Myles has enjoyed a constant supply :)

Just a few tips:

1. It's important to be meticulous when lining the tin. Smoothing out all the wrinkles will yield a better-looking cake.

2. Wrapping the outside of the tin in 2-3 layers of newspaper or brown paper prevents the edges from becoming overly dry during baking. NB: I promise the paper won't ignite in the oven!

3. To ensure that the cake stays fresh until Christmas, let it cool in the tin at least overnight before wrapping.

4. Avoid scraping the last of the mixture into the tin, as you will end up with cake mix without fruit on the top of your cake.

5. Bang the tin on the bench to eliminate all air pockets, before putting in the oven.

6. The cake is cooked when a skewer inserted in the middle comes out clean.

Shortening recipe:

This is the ideal method to grease your tin.

1 part flour to 4 parts copha. Melt the copha, add the flour, mix to form a paste. Store in a container in the fridge and reheat each time you need to use it.

Merry Christmas, everyone!

- 125 g sultanas
- 125 g currants
- 125 g raisins, chopped
- 45 g chopped red glacé cherries
- 60 g chopped mixed peel
- 45 g slivered almonds
- 50 ml brandy or sherry
- 30 g self-raising flour
- 125 g plain flour
- ¼ tsp grated nutmeg
- ¼ tsp ground ginger
- 125 g butter
- 125 g soft brown sugar
- 2 large eggs
- ¼ tsp lemon essence or finely grated lemon zest
- ¼ tsp almond essence
- ¼ tsp vanilla extract
- 20 g blanched almonds for decoration (optional)

Preheat oven to 150°C fan/170°C.

Preparing the 15 cm straight-sided, square-cornered tin.

Lining the tin:

Brush the tin sides and bottom with copha/flour paste. Let dry.

Line tin sides and base with baking paper and enclose the entire tin in 2 or 3 layers of newspaper/brown paper on the outside to come up 10 cm or so above the tin.

Tie securely with string.

For best results, fruit should be equal in size – raisins snipped 2-3 pieces, cherries 4-6 pieces.

Mix together all the fruits and nuts, sprinkle with sherry or brandy. Cover and leave for at least 1 hour, but preferably overnight or longer.

Sift together the flours and spices.

In a separate bowl, cream butter and sugar with the essences until smooth and lighter in colour.

Add the eggs, one at a time, beating well after each addition.

Add ⅓ of fruit, then ⅓ of flour mixture. Mix thoroughly. Repeat until all have been added.

The mixture should be stiff enough to support a wooden spoon.

Place the mixture into the prepared tin, decorate with blanched almonds, and bake for approximately 2 hours.

Allow cake to cool in the tin at least overnight to prevent cracking on the top.

https://youtu.be/Atbbcr13OQQ

Christmas mince pies

Makes 12

There is nothing quite like the smell of mince pies baking. They make the whole house smell like Christmas. They are also simple to make.

The trick to a good mince pie is getting the ratio of pastry to filling just right. To do this, you need to use a shallow pie tin or patty cake tin.

History of the mince pie:

The ingredients of the mince pies can be traced back to the return of the crusaders from the Holy Land. This was a combination of meats, fruits, and spices. In Tudor England, the pies were made from shredded meat, suet, and dried fruits. Spices such as cinnamon, cloves, and nutmeg were commonly added. Then, pies were larger than those served today, and usually oblong in shape.

In a recipe dating back from 1615, it is recommended to take a leg of mutton, and cutting the best bits off the bone, add mutton suet, pepper, salt, cloves, mace, currants, raisins, prunes, dates, and orange peel (https://en.wikipedia.org/wiki/Mince_pie). During the English civil war, the humble "Christmas Pie" was banned due to its ties with Catholicism. By the time of the Victorian era, the addition of meat to the pie had largely vanished, although suet was still used in both the filling and pastry.

There is lots to debate about the mince filling.

For many, the preparation of the filling starts months earlier, with the dried fruits and spices combined with alcohol and steeped in a dark place to develop the flavours. These make a rich and somewhat heavy pie.

My personal preference is a lighter combination of fruits and citrus zest. My recipe contains no alcohol. The fruit mince can be stored in the fridge for several weeks.

- 1 quantity of shortcrust pastry
- 2 cups mixed dried fruit
- 1 green apple, peeled and grated
- ¼ cup brown sugar
- 50 g butter, melted
- 2 tbl golden syrup
- ¼ tsp ground cinnamon
- Zest of 1 orange
- ½ cup orange juice
- ¼ cup slivered almonds

Preheat oven to 160°C fan/180°C.

Grease a 12-hole shallow baking tin.

Roll out pastry to 5 mm thick (or use frozen pastry sheets).

Cut out 12 x 10 cm rounds and ease into the tin.

Prick the base with a fork to prevent rising.

Cook for 10-12 minutes until golden. Allow to cool.

Combine remaining ingredients in a saucepan and simmer for 5-6 minutes until thick.

Allow to cool completely.

Fill each pastry shell with mince. Use leftover pastry to make a lattice.

Bake for 8-10 minutes until golden and crisp.

Store in an airtight container.

Gluten free Christmas pudding

Serves 15

Christmas time always comes quickly. The best way to deal with festive season stress is to be as prepared as you can, and be realistic with what you can do. I'm never going to have a perfectly designed lunch table with handmade name cards, homemade bonbons, and the perfect meal. But I can do a great meal.

As coeliacs, Christmas can be really difficult. Many of the festive foods are loaded with gluten, so not available for us. This recipe is so tasty, and so easy to convert, that no-one will know that they are eating gluten-free! So this year - volunteer to make the pudding for the family get together.

The beauty of traditional Christmas pudding is that it can be made months in advance - preferably on a cool spring day, so that you are not boiling away on the stove for hours when it's 35°C outside! It keeps well and once cooked can be stored in the pantry if plans change.

The recipe that I am sharing with you today is from Myles's side of the family. His grandmother took this from the Argus newspaper the year she got married - 1928. I have converted it to gluten-free (by replacing the breadcrumbs, flour and baking powder with GF alternatives - using the same measurements of ingredients). As this recipe was written in imperial measurements, I am going to give it to you in both imperial and metric. It is important to keep the measurement ratios as is, but rounding up or down slightly in the metric should not make too much difference. Be generous with the fruit and the nutmeg, as it certainly makes a better pudding. If you can't obtain dried figs, don't worry - the pudding will still be a great pudding, but in my humble opinion, it is the fig that makes this one really special.

This recipe will make a 2 kg pudding using an 8 cup pudding basin. I usually cook this recipe in 2 basins with each pudding weighing 1 kg. That way, I have one to share as a gift and one for our family lunch.

- 8 oz (227 g) butter
- 8 oz (227 g) sugar
- 12 oz (341 g) raisins
- 12 oz (341 g) sultanas
- 2 oz (57 g) peel
- 2 oz (57 g) chopped figs
- 7 oz (199 g) soft breadcrumbs (approx. 6 slices)
- 5 oz (142 g) plain flour
- 5 g xanthan gum
- 2 oz (57 g) chopped blanched almonds
- 1 tsp nutmeg
- ¼ tsp each of ground ginger, mixed spice, cinnamon, salt
- 1 tsp baking powder mixed into ½ cup milk
- 4 eggs
- Additional flour
- Unbleached calico, washed without soap

Using a stand mixer, beat together butter and sugar until the mixture becomes pale and the sugar is well incorporated. Add eggs one at a time and mix well in between.

Add all remaining ingredients and mix well.

Prepare the pudding cloth by rubbing extra flour into it. Use cloth, flour side away from the bowl, to line a pudding basin. Place mixture into cloth.

Gather cloth up and twist slightly. Using cooking twine, tightly seal the cloth. Ensure that all edges are above the knot.

Bring a large saucepan of water to a boil. Place a saucer upside down in the pot, and rest the pudding basin on the saucer. Ensure that all the cloth is on top of the pudding and none is in the water. The water should be halfway up the bowl. Place a tight-fitting lid on. Check the pot every half hour to ensure there is sufficient water in it. If you need to add more, boil the kettle and add the boiling water into the pot - being careful not to pour any into the pudding basin.

Steam for 5 hours. If you have halved the recipe and using a 4 cup basins steam for 3.5 hours.

Once the initial steaming is complete, remove pudding from the water, and allow to cool to room temperature. The pudding then needs to dry out. This can be done by storing in the fridge, or if you have a cool part of the house, they can be hung (this is more traditional).

Reheat the pudding by either steaming a further 2 hours (1 hour for the halved mixture). Serve with custard and brandy sauce.

https://youtu.be/copCsIxk-6w

Double choc raspberry muffins

Makes 12

It's pretty hard to resist the combination of rich dark chocolate and raspberries; they're definitely a match made in heaven. Personally, I find most commercial muffins too sweet, especially gluten-free varieties, as bakers often try to mask the lack of texture with additional sugar.

For these muffins, I've used the best quality Dutch cocoa I could purchase, along with dark chocolate chips. The slight bitterness of the chocolate pairs well with the tartness of the raspberries. Of course, you could use milk chocolate chips, but the muffins won't be as rich and decadent.

Dutch cocoa is a processed, unsweetened cocoa with a neutral pH. It has a mellow, smooth flavour and produces a darker result in your baking (and it doesn't come from the Netherlands!). It requires baking powder to create the rise in the muffins. Dutch cocoa also dissolves easily in liquids. If you choose to use natural cocoa powder, which is more acidic, you'll need to swap the baking powder for baking soda to achieve the same effect. In recipes where you're not after a rise, such as chocolate ice cream or hot chocolate, the two types of powder are interchangeable and the choice is up to personal preference. Understanding a bit about the chemistry of baking can lead to better results.

To ensure evenly-sized muffins, I prefer to use my 40ml ice cream scoop. This takes the guesswork out of distributing an even amount of batter into each muffin paper.

When it comes to presentation, there's an abundance of choices. I've used muffin papers here, but you could also use patty cases. There are thousands of different decorations, colours and patterns to choose from. Due to the lightness of these muffins, I recommend not using silver foil patty cases as the muffins can dry out a bit. Other than that, let your creativity run wild!

- 1½ cups plain flour
- 1 cup sugar
- ½ cup cocoa powder
- 1 tsp baking soda
- ½ tsp baking powder
- ¼ tsp salt
- ¼ tsp xanthan gum (only needed if using gluten-free flour)
- 1 tsp vanilla extract
- 2 eggs, beaten
- 100 g butter, melted
- 250 ml milk
- 150 g frozen raspberries
- ½ cup dark chocolate chips

Preheat oven to 180°C fan/200°C.

Place dry ingredients in a large bowl and whisk to combine. Make a well in the centre.

Keep aside 12 whole raspberries. Mix eggs, milk, remaining raspberries, vanilla and butter in a large jug.

Add milk mixture to dry ingredients. Mix well. Gently fold through chocolate chips.

Line a 12 patty tin with paper liners. Using an ice cream scoop, place mixture in liners. Top each muffin with a whole raspberry.

Bake for 20-25 minutes. Muffins are cooked when the top is gently pressed and springs back.

Cool on a wire rack.

https://youtu.be/cYdFx_YCSa8

Gluten free hot cross buns

Makes 12

Growing up, there were very few bakeries in our area, and none were open on Good Friday. Supermarkets only stocked Hot Cross Buns the week before Easter — unlike today, when commercial versions appear from Boxing Day onwards.

My mum and I would get up at 5:00 am on Good Friday to make these wonderful buns. As they came out of the oven, the most delightful aroma filled the kitchen and drifted out the door, drawing neighbours in to crowd around the table for a fresh bun. It became a local tradition that I continued for many years, and I still bake them fresh for our family. I'm a traditionalist — no choc chips! I prefer the slight tang of mixed peel, but you can leave it out if you prefer, though you'll lose the balance it brings against the sweetness and spices.

If you don't have access to the separate flours in this recipe, you can use 430 g of a commercial gluten-free plain flour — but results may vary. I recommend sticking to the individual flours for consistent results. I also like to use a proper piping bag for the crosses; a plastic bag with the corner cut off gives an inferior result. After all the effort, don't end up with "hot blob buns" at the last step! :)

- ¼ cup sugar
- 1 tsp salt
- 250 ml lukewarm milk
- 14 g dried yeast
- 155 g rice flour
- 90 g cornflour
- 85 g brown rice flour
- 75 g tapioca flour
- 25 g potato flour
- 1 tsp xanthan gum
- 1 tsp ground cinnamon
- ½ tsp ground nutmeg
- ¼ tsp ground cloves
- ¼ tsp ground allspice
- 1 egg, beaten
- 60 g butter, melted
- ½ cup sultanas
- ¼ cup currants
- 1 tbl mixed peel (optional)

Crosses:
- ½ cup cornflour
- 5-6 tbl water

Glaze:
- ½ cup sugar
- ¼ cup water
- ½ tsp cinnamon

Warm milk to 40°C in the microwave. Combine sugar, salt and milk in a small bowl. Add yeast and allow to stand until frothy.

In a large bowl, whisk together flours, xanthan gum and spices. Add egg and butter to the yeast mixture. Make a well in the flour and add the yeast mixture. Mix until combined.

Turn onto a lightly floured board and knead until smooth. Place in a lightly greased bowl. Cover with a damp tea towel and place in a warm place for 1 hour until doubled in size.

Tip the dough onto a lightly floured board. Knead in fruit to evenly distribute. Divide the dough into 12 x 80 g portions. Using a slightly oiled hand, roll into a ball. Place on a paper-lined tray and cover with a damp teatowel. Prove for another 30 minutes.

Preheat oven to 200°C fan/220°C.

To make crosses, mix together flour and water until smooth. Pipe crosses onto buns and bake for 12-15 minutes.

To make glaze, mix all ingredients together. Brush on the glaze while buns are still warm.

Allow to cool on a wire rack.

Serve with butter.

Gluten-free hot cross buns (Version 2)

Makes 8

For over 50 years, I have been making hot cross buns each Easter. I always used the same recipe that I made with my mum growing up - only changing to use dried yeast as fresh yeast has become difficult to source. Then when I was diagnosed as coeliac, I worked to convert mum's recipe to gluten free. In 2020 I released on my Youtube channel this recipe and I have received many fabulous comments from coeliacs around the world.

During the pandemic I became addicted to watching The Great British Bakeoff. It is a competition reality show, but the tips and techniques highlighted there are fantastic. I learnt more about proving yeasted products than I ever had with the comments provided by Paul Hollywood. One thing became clear, I needed a proving oven/drawer when I next updated my kitchen! In 2020 I also came across a fabulous blog by fellow coeliac, Cooking with Sass. Sass had become a home test baker for flour manufacturer FG Roberts and the results she shared looked amazing. I tried her white bread roll recipe and OMG! So in 2022 when she released a Hot Cross Bun recipe I decided I needed to try it.

The combination of successfully proving the buns in a regulated environment, along with using a bread flour and soaking the fruit is an absolute game changer! That's why, for the first time in the eleven years of doing this blog and Youtube videos I have gone back and done a Version 2 of a recipe.

This recipe is a combination of my mum's recipe and Sass's, using a couple of new techniques I have learned along the way.

As someone who always soaks fruit for Christmas Cakes, the need to soak the fruit for these buns was one of those "slap palm to forehead" moments. Of course, it plumps up the fruit and stops them drawing moisture from the dough. The result is a better, lighter, fluffier bun. Just make sure to pat dry the fruit before adding to the dough, soggy fruit can make your dough too wet.

Paul Hollywood taught me the importance of warming the milk before adding the yeast to activate it properly. Sass demonstrated that this needs to be between 40-45°C. Doing so, depending on the humidity and room temperature, the yeast blooms rapidly and fully within 5-8 minutes. I realised I often added the yeasty liquid to my dry ingredients too soon, before it had fully bloomed. You need to have a thick, "cream-like" top on the liquid, teeming with bubbles. If you're using a clear jug, you'll notice little bubbles on the side that resemble the top of a crumpet, filled with lots of tiny holes.

The other big change in this recipe is the flour. I now use a bread flour from Gluten Free World (formally known as FG Roberts). This bread mix contains Maize, Rice Fine Flour, Psyllium, soy isolate, soy flour enzyme active, dextrose, methocel K4M and salt. Psyllium is a crucial ingredient in gluten free bread making. It acts as a binder and gives the dough the elasticity which allows it to prove properly (and not collapse when exposed to cooler air.) Psyllium husk is a hydrocolloid - it binds with water to form a sticky elastic gel. This turns a bread batter into a bread dough. If you are interested more in how psyllium works check out https://theloopywhisk.com/2021/10/23/psyllium-husk-101

I can definitely recommend using a high sided baking tray, like a slice tin for these buns. The structure of the tin, and having them close together allows the buns to grow up, rather than spreading out.

I mention it in nearly every video, but the hardest part is always the waiting. And wait you must, especially after these have come out of the oven and you've glazed them. If you split them while still hot, they'll seem undercooked and doughy.

These buns are delicious at room temperature or lightly toasted the next day. Store them in an airtight container at room temperature. It's best to avoid refrigeration, as it tends to dry out the buns. I usually split the buns when they're cold and freeze them to enjoy over the next few months.

For the dough:
- 330 g Bread Mix (I use Gluten Free World)
- 80 g soft brown sugar
- 2 tsp ground cinnamon
- 1 tsp ground allspice
- ¼ tsp ground fresh nutmeg
- ¼ tsp ground ginger
- 1 tbl mixed peel or zest of an orange
- 400 g milk
- 6 g instant dry yeast
- 5 g white vinegar
- 30 g flavourless vegetable oil
- A pinch of salt flakes
- 50 g currants
- 50 g sultanas
- 50 g dried cranberries
- 1 egg, room temperature, beaten

For the crosses:
- 4 tbl plain flour (GF), combined with just enough water to be piped onto the buns.

For the glaze:
- 50 ml water
- 50 g soft brown sugar
- ¼ tsp cinnamon

Place dried fruit in a small bowl with a couple of tablespoons of warm water for at least 30 minutes.

Preheat oven to 200°C (fan-forced) and line a baking tray with baking paper.

Warm the milk and one tablespoon of sugar to 40-45°C. Add the yeast and gently mix into the milk. Cover and leave until the yeast starts to bloom.

In a large bowl of your stand mixer, combine the bread flour, salt, and spices.

Once the yeast blooms, add the vinegar, oil, egg, and remaining sugar and gently mix.

Make a well in the dry mixture and add the yeast mix.

Using the dough hook on your mixer, mix for 5 minutes until the flour is incorporated and the dough pulls away from the sides of the bowl. Scrape down the bowl. The dough will be quite sticky. Continue using the dough hook for another 3-5 minutes until the dough is smooth.

Drain the fruit and pat dry using paper towels. Add the fruit to the dough and mix for another 2-3 minutes until evenly distributed.

Place a piece of oiled cling film on your scales and weigh the dough. Divide by 8 to determine the weight of each bun, around 130 g each. Divide the dough into 8 even portions.

With lightly oiled hands, shape the portions into buns and place them almost touching on the prepared tin.

Cover with oiled cling film and allow the dough to rise in a warm spot until doubled in size, about 30 minutes using the dough proving function of your oven, or about 1 hour in a warm spot.

When the buns are ready to bake, mix the flour and water to make a thick paste. The mix should have the consistency of thick cream. Use a piping bag to pipe a cross onto the top of each bun.

Mist the buns lightly with water and place them into the pre-heated oven.

If your oven doesn't have a bread baking function, place a small oven-proof dish of water at the base of the oven to produce moisture while baking.

After 5 minutes, lower the temperature to 180°C and bake for a further 25-30 minutes. Time will vary depending on your oven.

To make the glaze, heat the glaze ingredients in a small saucepan until the sugar dissolves and the glaze bubbles.

Gently brush the glaze over the buns with a pastry brush while they are still hot.

Allow the buns to come to room temperature before splitting open. Serve with plenty of butter :)

https://youtu.be/fuoEbMgvpLs

Sticky date pudding

Serves 4-6

As the autumn leaves start to colour, the mornings start with a fresh crispness, and the nights are getting colder, it's time to start thinking about comfort food. These are the dishes that warm us up from our toes and bring back memories of childhood - licking the spoon or the beaters, getting chocolate all over our faces, and the wonderful baking smells drifting from the kitchen.

For Myles, one of his favourite comfort foods is sticky date pudding. It's not too sweet, yet light and fluffy, dripping with butterscotch sauce. Often, I replace the butterscotch sauce with loads of golden syrup - just as sweet but with fewer calories. The secret to the lightness of this pudding is the bicarbonate of soda.

Bicarbonate of soda is a leavening agent. It reacts with acidic components in batters, releasing carbon dioxide, which causes expansion of the batter and forms the characteristic texture and grain in pancakes, cakes, quick breads, soda bread, and other baked and fried foods. Acidic compounds that induce this reaction include phosphates, cream of tartar, lemon juice, yoghurt, buttermilk, cocoa, vinegar, etc. Sodium bicarbonate can be substituted for baking powder provided sufficient acid reagent is also added to the recipe. Many forms of baking powder contain sodium bicarbonate combined with calcium acid phosphate, sodium aluminium sulphate or cream of tartar.

Heat causes sodium bicarbonate to act as a raising agent by releasing carbon dioxide. The carbon dioxide production starts at temperatures above 80°C. Since the reaction does not occur at room temperature, mixtures (cake batter, etc.) can be allowed to stand without rising until they are heated in the oven. (https://en.wikipedia.org/wiki/Sodium_bicarbonate)

I hope you enjoy this recipe. Any leftovers keep well in the fridge for a few days and can be reheated in the microwave or steam oven.

- 185 g pitted dates, roughly chopped
- 1 tsp bicarbonate of soda
- 300 ml water
- 60 g unsalted butter, softened
- 185 g caster sugar
- 2 large eggs
- 200 g plain flour (GF)
- 1 tsp vanilla extract

Butterscotch Sauce:
- 240 g brown sugar
- 250 g butter
- 30 ml thickened cream

Preheat oven to 165°C fan/180°C.

Grease 4 x 250 ml ramekin dishes, or 6 x 175 ml ramekin dishes.

Combine dates and water in a small saucepan and bring to the boil. Remove from heat and add bicarbonate of soda.

Cream butter and sugar until light and fluffy. Add eggs one at a time, beating well to incorporate.

Fold in flour.

Stir in vanilla and the slightly cooled date mixture.

Spoon into ramekins, and cook for 25 minutes, or until cooked.

Butterscotch Sauce:

Combine all ingredients in a small saucepan, stir over heat until sugar is dissolved. Simmer, stirring constantly for 5 minutes. Serve warm.

https://youtu.be/xuqX7cJ1vGU

Tropical tiramisu

Makes 6

Christmas is a time to treat those you love. Christmas in Australia is such a mixture of Northern Hemisphere imagery, summer heat, and family traditions all rolled up together. My family always have a baked ham, hot roasted vegetables and other hot dishes for the main course, but usually start with cold prawns and other seafood and finish with homemade Shiraz jelly, tropical tiramisu, and hot Christmas pudding. All the while, we sit next to a decorated Christmas tree, surrounded by Christmas cards depicting snow, waving in the breeze from the air conditioner, trying to combat both the heat of the day and that emanating from the oven!

The recipe I've chosen here can be made in a large lasagne dish or in individual glasses. I've used tropical flavours easily found in Australia at Christmas, but the fruit options are endless. Poached peaches, pomegranate seeds, and stewed berries would also be delicious, and provide some interesting colours. Just a note – I've used fresh passionfruit. If you use a tin of passionfruit pulp, you'll need to strain the pulp as the contents of the tin are far too watery. The juice can be added to the orange juice if desired, and just use the pulp and seeds for the fruit layer.

Traditional tiramisu recipes include beaten egg in the cream layer, making for a richer layer. Due to the climatic conditions in Australia, I prefer not to include the raw egg unless I'm serving this dish at home and can be very certain that it will be eaten straight from the fridge within 24 hours of being made. If you want to add the egg, beat 1 extra-large egg and ¼ cup of caster sugar until thick and creamy. Fold this into the cream mixture with the mascarpone. This will make the cream mixture thinner and unable to be piped.

To soak the biscuits in this recipe, I've used orange juice. Pineapple juice could also be used; however, I recommend diluting it a bit with some orange juice due to its acidity. Adding Galliano or a coconut-flavoured liqueur is also lovely depending on your family's preferences. If you add alcohol, reduce the juice to 125ml. Take care when dipping the biscuits – it's a fine balancing act between softening the biscuit and ending up with a soggy mess.

- 450 ml thickened cream
- 40 g icing sugar
- Zest of 1 lime
- 250 g mascarpone
- 4 mangoes, diced
- 200 ml passionfruit pulp (approx. 8 fruits)
- 1 cup orange juice
- 200 g savoiardi biscuits
- 125 ml Galliano or coconut-flavored liqueur (optional)
- 6 x 250 ml serving glasses

In a large bowl whisk together cream, icing sugar and lime zest until stiff. Gently fold in mascarpone.

In a flat dish combine juice and alcohol (if using). Taking only one biscuit at a time, dip both sides of the biscuit in the juice mix, and then place on a board. Continue until 4 or 5 biscuits have been dipped. Cut the biscuits to form a layer on the bottom of each glass.

Gently spoon a layer of mango into each glass.

Spoon ½ a passionfruit into each glass.

Spoon or pipe approximately ⅓ cup of the cream mixture into each glass.

Repeat by adding another layer of dipped biscuits.

Repeat the layers of passionfruit and mango.

Top with the cream mixture and place in the fridge for 6 hours or overnight.

Prior to serving, place ½ tsp of passionfruit on each glass.

https://youtu.be/6_8Q-859pj8

Baked ham with maple syrup & mustard glaze

Serves 10+

Christmas food traditions often revolve around shared dishes that are elevated with extra flourishes. These flourishes transform everyday food into a celebration, which is particularly true for a baked ham. This centerpiece dish is a family favourite. My younger brother insists on bringing one each year, and every year he experiments with a different glaze. They all oscillate around savoury and sweet themes, the sugar caramelizing into a rich, sticky contrast against the salty meat underneath.

When preparing the ham, it's crucial to leave as much fat on the leg as possible when removing the skin. The fat, coupled with the glaze, contributes to caramelization and ensures the meat remains moist and succulent.

Given the ham usually weighs between 3 to 8 kg, leftovers are inevitable. To preserve your ham, store it in a ham bag or wrap it in a damp tea towel in the fridge. Before using the bag, soak it in a mixture of 1 litre of water and 2 tablespoons of white vinegar. Squeeze out the excess liquid, leaving the bag damp. For the best results, repeat this process every few days. Remember to wrap your ham loosely to allow air circulation and store it in the coolest part of the fridge soon after serving. The bone can be frozen for up to 6 months and is perfect for making pea and ham soup.

The skin, carefully removed, is not ideal for making crackling due to the smoking process that the ham has undergone. However, this doesn't deter my little brother from trying!

Exercise caution when serving the ham. Cloves have a very strong flavour and can be unpleasant if bitten into. Cloves are the dried flower buds from the clove tree. They have some medicinal uses, including treatment for toothache pain, stress relief, and inflammation reduction for conditions like arthritis. However, they are very strong in flavour. Most medicinal applications use clove oil or ground cloves.

- 1 whole leg ham on the bone
- 100 g brown sugar
- 80 ml maple syrup
- 80 ml honey
- 1 tbl Dijon mustard
- Whole cloves

In a small bowl, combine sugar, maple syrup, honey and mustard.

Preheat oven to 170°C fan/190°C

Line a large baking dish with 2 layers of non-stick baking paper. Put a rack on the paper.

Use a sharp knife to cut around the shank of the ham, about 10cm from the end. Run a knife under the rind around edge of ham. Gently lift the rind off in 1 piece by running your fingers between the rind and the fat.

Score the fat in a diamond pattern, about 5mm deep. Stud the centres of the diamonds with cloves. Transfer onto the rack in the prepared dish.

Brush with ⅓ of the maple syrup glaze. Bake, brushing with glaze every 25 minutes, for 1 hour 30 minutes. You may need to cover the shank of the leg with tin foil during the cooking process if it is drying out too much.

https://youtu.be/G9ePmqdivsA

Pea and ham soup

Serves 4-6

On cold winter nights, there is nothing quite like coming home to a steaming plate of pea and ham soup. This has always been one of my absolute favourites, and my mum's is pretty hard to beat!

This hearty soup is naturally gluten-free and uses simple ingredients. The only tricky part is leaving it to settle overnight to remove the fat and taking the meat off the bone. I'm sure that there are readers who use bacon bones and pieces of bacon in their soup, but for my money, nothing beats the smoky flavour imparted by the ham hock.

Ham hocks are the shin of the pig. They have a rubbery skin, which is discarded at the final stage of cooking. The meat is succulent and slightly salty. This means no added salt is required.

There are two types of split peas - yellow and green. I always use the yellow for this soup. There is no taste difference, but Mum always uses yellow, and I see no reason to change. Split peas are high in protein and low in fat. They are also high in fibre (25 g of fibre per 100 g portion).

- 1 smoked ham hock
- 400 g split peas
- 1 brown onion, diced
- Water, as needed

Place all ingredients in a large, solid-based stockpot. Cover with water and bring to the boil. Simmer for an hour and a half.

Cool to room temperature, then refrigerate overnight. The next day, using a flat spoon, skim off the fat. Remove the ham hock, peel and discard the skin from the ham hock. Remove all meat from the bone, chopping into small morsels. Return the meat to the pot. Stir well. Bring back to the boil and simmer for 10 minutes.

Serve with crusty bread or damper.

https://youtu.be/3fasGAnyTyw

Gluten free pumpkin soup & cheesy damper

Serves 4

I certainly love winter. I love layers of clothing - possum wool socks, scarves and of course hats!

I also love the comfort food that comes into its own at this time of year. As nights get colder, settling down to a piping hot bowl of soup just makes you feel good. Perfectly accompanied by a cheesy damper to dunk into a bowl of steaming pumpkin soup.

There are two ways to make this soup - the weekender and the weekday. On weekends when you have the time, roasting the diced pumpkin brings out the sweetness and makes a really delicious soup. The reality for most of us during the week is that we need dinner served to the family quickly. This soup is also lovely when made by boiling the ingredients until soft and then blending. The sweetness isn't enhanced in this method, but the comfort food effect remains.

A good soup always starts with a good stock. I am really struck by how many "ready made" stocks there are out there on the market. Many of them filled with preservatives and thickeners, many of which are not gluten-free. It's crazy - when making stock is just so simple and cheap. Any leftover stock can be frozen for up to 3 months.

The stock does need to be prepared the day before, so if you are wanting to make this soup quickly and have no stock handy, you can use commercially prepared stock in this recipe, but the best results and flavour are achieved by making your own.

Stock:
- 3 chicken carcasses
- 1 tbl black peppercorns
- 2 bay leaves
- 1 carrot
- 1 white onion, peeled
- 2 celery sticks
- 3 l water

Soup:
- 1 kg pumpkin, diced
- 1 onion, chopped
- 1 large potato, diced
- 2 l chicken stock
- Sour cream, to serve

Cheesy damper:
- 3 cups self-raising flour
- 1 cup grated cheese
- 60 g butter, cubed
- 1 tsp salt
- ¼ tsp cayenne pepper
- 1 cup milk
- Juice of ½ lemon
- Extra flour (for kneading)

Stock:

Place all ingredients into a large pot, simmer for 2-3 hours, then let cool and leave overnight in the fridge. Next day, skim any fat from the top and strain.

Soup:

Roast pumpkin in a little olive oil for 45 minutes at 160°C fan/180°C. Allow to cool.

Combine roasted pumpkin (or raw pumpkin if time poor), raw potato, onion and stock in a large pot. Bring to the boil and simmer for 20 minutes until the potato is cooked. Blend with a stick blender or food processor until smooth.

Serve with sour cream.

Cheesy damper:

Preheat oven to 210°C fan/190°C.

Combine flour, salt, and cayenne pepper in a large bowl. Add butter and rub in until it resembles fine breadcrumbs. Add cheese and mix.

Sour the milk by adding lemon juice.

Add ¾ cup of milk to flour mixture and using a knife combine until a firm scone dough consistency is achieved (You may need to add more of the milk).

Knead dough on a lightly floured surface until smooth. Place onto a non-stick tray and pat into a circle shape, approximately 1.5 cm thick.

Using a knife, cut through the dough most of the way to score into 8 wedges.

Brush top with a little milk and bake for 25-30 mins until golden brown and cooked in the middle.

https://youtu.be/jSBZ2fgqYyU

Yorkshire pudding

Makes 12

It's hard to remember when Yorkshire puddings became a staple in my house - they were not part of my upbringing even though Mum's family served many traditional English dishes, having come out from Cornwall in the 1850s seeking their fortune in the gold rush.

Yorkshire puddings were first documented in 1747 by Hannah Glasse in her book The Art of Cookery Made Plain and Easy. Prior to that, a very similar dish named dripping pudding was popular. They are similar to the American dish "Dutch baby pancakes". They traditionally used the fat dripping from the roasting meat and were served as a first course with gravy to help "fill you up" before the more expensive course of meat and vegetables.

There is even a National Yorkshire Pudding Day - the first Sunday in February! It's a bit too hot here in Australia in February to be baking a roast, but that doesn't stop us enjoying them anytime we are having a roast, especially roast beef.

I prefer to bake 12 individual pieces rather than a large loaf - easier to serve out. The change from gluten-based flour to gluten-free has not impacted this dish at all. No one seems to notice - the GF store-bought blend I use is White Wings brand. They rise up, fluffy on the inside and crisp on the outside - just waiting to be smothered in lots of gravy.

The trick is to have the pan and oil really hot and the batter at room temperature to get the perfect result.

- 170 g plain flour (GF)
- 300 ml milk
- 2 eggs, room temperature
- 30 g butter, melted
- 7 g sea salt
- Pepper, to taste
- Vegetable oil

Preheat oven to 210°C fan/230°C.

Place a tbl of vegetable oil in each section of a 12-hole non-stick muffin tin and place on the top shelf of the oven until very hot, almost smoking.

To make the batter, place the flour into a bowl and beat in the eggs until smooth. Gradually add the milk and melted butter. Continue to beat until the mix is completely lump-free. Season with salt and pepper.

As soon as you take the tray from the oven, pour the batter into the tin, to three-quarters full (it should sizzle) and immediately put back into the oven.

Bake until the Yorkshire puddings are well risen, golden brown, and crisp, 20 to 25 minutes. Don't open the oven door until the end or they might collapse.

Serve with roast beef and lots of gravy.

https://youtu.be/gJ4umF957ZQ

European Quartet

For many Australians, travelling to Europe is seen as a rite of passage. Many Australians have their ancestral roots in Europe, with European settlement in Australia starting in 1788. My first European adventure was in late 1990, where I backpacked with my then boyfriend around Europe for 9 months. Frankfurt am Main was our base, in the newly united Federal Republic of Germany.

Since then, I have been fortunate to visit mainland Europe on a number of occasions, and England three times. The foods of Spain and France are always the highlight of our trips. Myles and I plan our holiday around local market days, cooking classes, and cafes tucked away in small villages. These experiences have influenced every aspect of my cooking, and I have only scratched the surface of what these cuisines have to offer.

My mum's family arrived in Australia in the 1850s, part of the wave of Cornish tin miners who came seeking their fortunes during the Victorian gold rush. They settled in Bendigo. One of the things they brought with them was the Cornish pasty - a simple, practical food that became a family favourite.

For me, the pasty represents more than just a meal—it's a connection to my family's past. The tradition of making pasties has been passed down through generations. I remember being at my grandma's, where no matter how young you were, you always had a part in making them. And it was never just enough for one meal—you always made a big batch, enough to feed the family for days. It's a dish that's always carried with it a sense of home.

So, for me, the European Quartet is Germany, Spain, France, and England.

Marché des Lices on a bustling Saturday market day in Rennes, France

Baked pears

Serves 2

As the days grow shorter and the nights colder, comfort foods truly come into their own. Baked desserts are a special treat in our house, reserved for weekends or very special occasions.

Autumn is the prime time to cook with pears and apples, as both fruits are in season. There are many varieties of pears to choose from. Although any can be used in this recipe, the Beurré Bosc variety is preferred. Originating from France, this variety features a white, dense, crisp flesh that maintains its shape well when cooked, making it perfect for poaching or baking. It is identifiable by its rusty brown skin. Our friend, Long, amusingly calls them "ugly pears," as they are often the last ones left in the communal workplace fruit bowl.

This recipe can be easily scaled up to suit the number of guests you're serving. As a rule of thumb, I serve two halves per person.

As this recipe produces a caramel sauce, extra care is required during handling. After all, it is boiling sugar and can cause severe burns if spilled onto your skin. The final baking step must be monitored closely as, depending on your oven, the caramel can easily burn. We are aiming for a deep, golden color.

- ½ tsp vanilla paste
- 75 g caster sugar
- 20 g butter
- Juice of 1 lemon
- 2 Beurré Bosc pears
- Shaved almonds, toasted (for garnish)
- Whipped cream, to serve

Preheat oven to 200°C fan/220°C.

Place sugar, vanilla, butter and lemon juice in baking dish. Place in oven until butter has melted. Stir well.

Split each pear into two lengthways. Using a spoon, gently remove core. Place pears face down in the dish. Cover with foil and bake for 25 minutes.

Carefully turn over pears. Leave the dish uncovered and bake until soft (20-25 minutes).

Allow the dish to stand for a few minutes before serving. Serve with cream and toasted almonds.

Notes:

* Beurré Bosc pears' white flesh is denser, crisper and smoother than that of other pears. But you can use other pears.

* Generally serve one pear (two halves) per person. This recipe is easy to scale up to serve more people.

* Monitor the last few minutes of cooking carefully as the caramel can darken quickly, and you don't want to burn the sauce.

* Maybe swirl cream into caramel sauce (which will make it more of a butterscotch).

* Let cool just a little before serving, as it will be very hot. But don't let cool as the caramel will set hard.

Basque cheesecake

Serves 16

There are significant moments in life where you have to pinch yourself to make sure you're not dreaming. October 2018, I found myself in one such moment. My wonderful partner Myles had arranged for us to spend two fantastic days studying at the MIMO San Sebastian Cooking School in San Sebastian, Spain. For two remarkable days, Mateo guided us in mastering the cooking techniques used in the Basque regions of modern-day Spain and France.

The recipe provided here for the Basque Cheesecake has been slightly tweaked from Mateo's original to make it gluten-free. It is crucial to include the small amount of flour required, as this helps reduce or eliminate the "weeping" that can occur from the cheesecake once it has cooled. The ideal texture has each slice featuring a thin ribbon in the centre that remains "gooey".

When baking, it is important to use a good quality 20 cm springform tin. Don't forget to trim the baking paper used to line the tin to about 3 cm above the edge of the tin. If any paper protrudes much further, it may burn in the oven, risking burnt paper falling onto the cooking cheesecake.

Determining when the cheesecake is cooked can be a little tricky. The cheesecake will turn a golden brown. To test if it's ready, give the tin a small shake. If the mixture moves in a single wave, it is ready. However, if there are multiple ripples, it needs a few more minutes in the oven.

This is a very rich cheesecake, and I recommend serving small portions—you can always go back for seconds.

- 1 kg cream cheese, at room temperature
- 7 medium eggs, at room temperature
- 400 g sugar
- 1 tbl plain flour (GF)
- 500 ml cream

Preheat oven to 220°C fan/240°C.

Using a stand mixer, beat the cream cheese to soften.

Break eggs into a small bowl and beat well, ensuring you don't incorporate too much air into the mixture. Add the eggs to the cream cheese and mix well. Add the sugar and mix thoroughly. Then add the cream and the flour. Use a stick blender to combine the ingredients well, aiming to achieve a smooth consistency.

Line a 20 cm springform pan with baking paper. Ensure the paper extends about 3 cm above the pan, as the batter will rise during baking. Trim the paper as necessary.

Pour the batter into the pan, place it in the centre of a baking tray, and then into the oven. Bake for 40-50 minutes. The top should be dark brown and display a slight wobble, or a single wave, when moved. If you prefer a firmer cheesecake, add another 5 minutes, but be cautious as they can burn easily. While you could check with a skewer in the centre, traditionally the middle is a bit gooey.

Remove the cake from the oven and allow it to sit in the tin for at least an hour. Carefully remove the sides of the tin and peel back the paper. Lift the cake from the pan and place it onto a large serving plate.

https://youtu.be/i_aaKE3xrJo

Cannelé

Makes 18

I was first introduced to Cannelés by my bobbin lace teacher, Robyn Keatley. Robyn had experimented with gluten-free flour and made them for supper during class — they were pretty good! She used silicone moulds but was searching for traditional fluted trays, which sparked my own hunt. The right tools not only make cooking easier but also enhance the final dish — there's a reason these large, fluted thimble shapes have been used for generations.

In 2018, I spent time in the Basque region of France, staying in the walled town of St Jean Pied de Port, a beautiful place steeped in history at the foothills of the Pyrenees. It remains a major stop for pilgrims walking the Camino de Santiago. One of its artisan shops was home to a specialist Cannelé baker who offered nine different flavours, including savoury ones. Myles, of course, tried them all! In my "best French", I spoke with the baker, who stressed the importance of using the best tins you could afford and a special release spray — something I sadly haven't been able to source in Australia.

I purchased two traditional copper tins, but despite several attempts, I've yet to successfully season them so the Cannelés don't stick. Meanwhile, my heavy solid metal tray, bought locally, has worked perfectly every time. A simple trick to help prevent sticking is to chill the tray before brushing with melted butter. You can use muffin tins if needed, but the cooking time will vary due to the volume. You're aiming for a deep, toffee-coloured crust, not a pale one.

Many recipes recommend preparing the batter at least 24 hours before baking — and it's just as crucial for gluten-free versions. The batter will separate as it rests, but this allows the flours to absorb moisture and the flavours to develop. Stir gently before using. I wouldn't leave the batter longer than three days, though, as the texture becomes noticeably denser over time, particularly when using bread flour in traditional versions.

One last word of warning: unlike most gluten-free baking where you cool goods in the tin, with Cannelés you must turn them out immediately onto a wire rack. If you leave them to cool inside, the caramelised sugar will glue them in place and cause tears — literally and figuratively!

Myles' favourite was the classic rum and vanilla Cannelé, which I've adapted here to be gluten-free. When eaten warm, the outside is crisp and caramelised, while the inside is light, fluffy, and slightly custardy.

- 600 ml whole milk
- 1 vanilla bean
- 30 g soft butter
- 180 g caster sugar
- 100 g plain flour (GF)
- 3 eggs
- Fat pinch of sea salt
- 80 ml dark rum

Day 1:

Place milk in a saucepan.

Split vanilla pod and scrape out the seeds. Add seeds and pod to the milk and heat gently. Once it is just simmering, add the butter and remove pan from the heat.

In a large jug combine sugar, flour, eggs and salt. Using a spatula, so as not to incorporate too much air, add the milk. Then add the rum, mixing well.

Using a fine mesh sieve, sieve the batter back into the pot. Sieve the batter again back into the jug. Return the vanilla pod to the jug. Allow the batter to come to room temperature, and then refrigerate for at least 24 hours. Batter can be stored for 48 hours if required.

Baking day:

Preheat oven to 230°C fan/250°C.

Chill Cannelé pan and then brush with melted butter.

Remove the vanilla pod from the batter. The batter will have separated, so gently remix, again without incorporating too much air.

Fill cannelé tins to about 1 cm from the top, to allow for the batter to rise during baking.

Bake for 15 minutes, then turn the oven down to 180°C fan/200°C and bake for another 30 minutes.

Turn immediately onto a cooling tray.

https://youtu.be/R45rhuLIBJc

Cherry cheesecake

Serves 10

Although it's hard to believe that summer is just around the corner when looking out of my window today. Summer is signalled by many things: days getting longer and warmer, gardens in bloom, football finals over, and of course the arrival of cherries at farmers' markets and grocery stores. There is nothing like the taste of fresh cherries and the bright colour they bring to the table.

So when fresh cherries are not available, don't despair! Tinned cherries make a fabulous substitute in this recipe (and have a bonus in that you don't have to remove the pits!).

Generally, there are two types of cheesecake - baked and set. This recipe is a set cheesecake. But even amongst set cheesecakes, there is variation as to the degree of "setness". In this recipe, the filling is quite soft. You could add a couple of gelatine sheets softened in cold water to the filling before folding in the cream if you wanted a firmer filling.

As I have used tinned cherries to make this cheesecake, I have thickened the juice with arrowroot and used it with the topping. In this case, you CANNOT use cornflour instead, as cornflour will turn the cherry juice a disappointing shade of grey and cloudy. Arrowroot is a generic name for a group of flours that includes Tapioca flour. As a coeliac, I use Tapioca flour all the time due to its "holding" properties in baking.

This is a special occasion dessert. It is very heavy on the dairy, so don't be too generous with your portion sizes.

- 200 g butter
- 1 tsp ground ginger
- 350 g plain gluten-free biscuits
- 250 g cream cheese
- 2 tbl kirsch
- ½ cup pure icing sugar
- 1¼ cups crème fraîche
- 1¼ cups cream
- 500 g fresh cherries or 400g tin cherries, drained and juice reserved
- 1 tbl arrowroot (tapioca flour) * see note above

Crush biscuits and ground ginger in a food processor until they become fine crumbs. Place them into a 22 cm springform tin. Add melted butter and mix until combined. If there are any larger bits of broken biscuit, remove them at this point for an even crust.

Using a straight-sided glass, press the biscuit mixture evenly around the sides and base. This is a bit fiddly, but it is worth taking the time to get this right. Chill until firm - approximately 30 minutes.

Using a food processor, beat cream cheese, icing sugar, and 1 tablespoon of kirsch until smooth. Add crème fraîche and mix well (If adding gelatine, this is the time to do it).

In a separate bowl, whip cream until stiff.

Gently fold the cream into the filling.

Gently pour the filling into the prepared biscuit case, smoothing out the top. Chill for at least an hour.

Pit fresh cherries if using.

When you are ready to serve, toss the remaining kirsch with cherries.

Unclip the springform tin sides and gently remove the cheesecake. Place the cheesecake onto a serving plate. Pile cherries on top.

If you have used tinned cherries, mix 1 tablespoon of arrowroot with reserved juice. Gently heat, stirring minimally until thickened. Allow to cool and pour over cherries.

https://youtu.be/8Z8hYia55DY

Chocolate raspberry mousse

Serves 4

It's probably no surprise that the French were the first to create mousse. Some articles even credit the post-Impressionist painter Henri Toulouse-Lautrec with its invention in the late 19th century. In French, 'mousse' means 'froth' or 'foam'. Chocolate remains the most popular flavour for all ages.

Let's talk chocolate! There are eight main types: Baking, Bittersweet, Semisweet, Sweet, Milk, White, Cocoa Powder, Couverture, and Cocoa Nibs. For mousse, the best options are couverture or bittersweet. Couverture contains at least 32% cocoa butter, making it glossy and easy to temper. Bittersweet has a high percentage of cocoa solids and gives a rich flavour. Cocoa butter is crucial — it lowers viscosity, sets to a brittle snap, contracts for easy mould release, and melts beautifully in the mouth.

Chocolate can seize for three main reasons: overheating (especially in a microwave), contact with water, or insufficient liquid in recipes using high-cocoa chocolate. If a little steam gets in while melting, don't despair — the egg mixture and raspberry purée will still bring the mousse together. (More on saving seized chocolate: https://food52.com/blog/14453-what-to-do-when-your-chocolate-seizes.)

Temperature matters. All ingredients should be at the same temperature when combined. Let the chocolate cool toward room temperature as you whip the cream; otherwise, the cream will melt and the mousse will become heavy.

Adding raspberry purée adds complexity: you first taste raspberry, then the deep chocolate flavour unfolds as the mousse melts in your mouth. That's cocoa butter at work. This is a sophisticated dessert you can prepare a day ahead. If it's been refrigerated for more than an hour, remove it at least 30 minutes before serving, so the cocoa butter can properly melt and deliver maximum richness.

- 125 g raspberries
- 60 g caster sugar
- 100 g chocolate (66-70% cocoa solids)
- 3 egg yolks
- ½ tsp vanilla extract
- 150 ml thickened cream
- 1 tbl icing sugar

In a food processor blend raspberries and 50 ml of cream. Purée until broken down.

Place a fine mesh sieve over a small saucepan and pour the raspberries into the sieve. Push the purée through using a spatula and then discard the seeds.

Heat the mixture until just starting to steam and remove it from the heat. Set aside to cool slightly.

Break up the chocolate and place in a heatproof bowl. Place the bowl over a pot of simmering water, making sure that the water does not touch the bowl. Gently heat the chocolate, stirring occasionally until the chocolate has melted. Place the bowl to the side, keeping warm.

In a heatproof bowl, mix together caster sugar, egg yolks and 2 tablespoon warm water. Place over simmering water making sure the water doesn't touch the bowl. Whisk together for 8 minutes until the mixture turns pale, thickens and forms ribbons when you lift the whisk.

Gently fold through the melted chocolate until well combined. Stir in the raspberry mixture.

In a separate bowl whisk together vanilla, remaining cream and icing sugar until stiff peaks form. Fold in ⅓ of the chocolate mixture. Then fold in the remaining chocolate mixture to achieve a smooth consistency with no white patches, being careful not to overmix.

Divide into 4 dishes. Cover with cling wrap and refrigerate for at least 1 hour. Remove from the fridge 30 minutes before serving. Top with a raspberry and chocolate shards to serve.

Coconut macaroons

Makes 36-42

Who doesn't love a sweet treat to enjoy with coffee!

These coconut macaroons are quick to prepare, delicious, and naturally gluten-free but I must warn you - it's hard to stop at one!

These are one of Myles' childhood favourites. His sister Fiona recounts the story of using an egg cup dipped in water to get the rounded shape. Myles doesn't remember this, but does remember eating as many as possible!

There are a few variations:
- Replace the vanilla extract with a tbl rum.
- Add the zest of a lime when adding the coconut.
- Dip half the macaroon, after baking, in melted dark chocolate and allow to cool on a wire rack.

- 4 cups shredded coconut
- ½ cup sugar
- 2 large egg whites
- Pinch of salt
- 1 tbl cornflour
- 1 tsp vanilla extract

Preheat oven to 180°C fan/200°C.

Line a baking sheet with baking paper.

Place shredded coconut into a food processor bowl and pulse several times until coconut is finely chopped (not into coconut flour, but into small, rice-sized bits).

In a large bowl, whisk together egg whites, sugar and salt until smooth. Whisk in cornflour and vanilla. Stir in coconut, making sure the entire mixture is an even consistency.

Drop rounded teaspoons (so roughly 2 teaspoon balls, if using a standard measure) onto a baking paper lined baking sheet.

Bake for 10-15 minutes, until golden on the bottom and top.

Cool on baking sheet for 5 minutes, then transfer to wire rack to cool completely.

Store in an airtight container.

https://youtu.be/-aH0kanBDfI

Crema Catalana

Serves 6

Myles and I first cooked this recipe on our day @Barcelonacooking, which was a fantastic introduction to Spanish ingredients and cooking. After a guided tour of the fabulous Mercat de la Boqueria with Candido, we returned to the school to make a meal including Tomato Bread, Strawberry Gazpacho, Paella and for dessert Crema Catalana. This simple dessert with dramatic flair is a showstopper at any dinner table. It has already become a favourite and is simple to prepare - Myles has even made it! In fact, when touring around France later that trip we needed to stop at a kitchen equipment shop to purchase a cooking butane torch as our accommodation didn't have one in the kitchen, and Myles wanted to serve this for our travelling companions, Bev and Lindsay Noss.

- 3 egg yolks
- 500 ml milk
- 80 g sugar
- 20 g corn flour
- 1 vanilla pod, split to remove seeds
- Zest of 1 lemon

Whisk egg yolks, sugar, and corn flour in a large bowl until thick and creamy.

In a large pot, add milk, vanilla pod, vanilla seeds and lemon zest, then bring to a simmer on low heat.

Strain milk into egg mixture and whisk together.

Return custard to the pot, and on gentle heat return to boil, stirring constantly.

At the first sign of bubbles, test custard consistency. The custard is ready when you can draw a clean line through it on the back of a spoon using your finger. If it passes the test remove from heat and carefully ladle into ramekins.

Allow to cool, then refrigerate.

Before serving sprinkle sugar onto each ramekin, then caramelise with a kitchen butane torch. Serve immediately.

https://youtu.be/p9UNK_0ibwQ

Gluten free crêpes

Makes 8

Crêpes are a versatile base for so many recipes, both sweet and savoury. The batter can be made ahead of time and stored in the fridge for up to 2 days - when ready to use, just bring to room temperature and whisk well. You can also make the crêpes ahead of time, and store for up to 2 hours wrapped in a moist cloth.

I like to use them as a special dessert for guests, or a celebratory breakfast, served with fresh berries, a drizzle of maple syrup and ice cream.

As with all gluten-free cooking, you can use a commercially prepared plain flour mix. I find that the differences between brands can make for inconsistent results. That is why I have specified the three staple flour ratios: tapioca, potato, and rice. This way, I can guarantee a great result every time.

To make crêpes, I recommend using a crêpe pan and crêpe spatula. Using the right equipment certainly makes a difference.

- 20 g tapioca flour
- 40 g potato flour
- 110 g rice flour (total 170 g plain flour blend)
- ½ tsp salt
- 2 eggs, at room temperature
- 20 g butter, melted and cooled
- 330 ml milk, at room temperature

Combine all the dry ingredients in a large bowl. In a smaller bowl, whisk milk, eggs and butter together.

Make a well in the dry ingredients, and pour in the milk mixture. Whisk together well.

Heat a crêpe pan to 200°C. Lightly grease the pan with butter. Carefully pour 1/3 cup of batter into the centre of the pan, swirling the pan to get an even distribution.

Cook over a medium heat until the edges and underside of the crêpe are lightly golden (approximately 90 seconds). With a wide spatula, carefully turn the crêpe over and cook until lightly golden (approx 30 seconds).

Repeat with remaining batter.

https://youtu.be/nteyGFLhZpo

Gluten free gingerbread

Makes 20

There is something about the aroma of cinnamon, cloves, nutmeg - they all say "It's Christmas" and there is nothing better than having the whole house infiltrated with wafts of Christmas baking. Of course, here in Australia, it's mid-summer at Christmas, and so most of my Christmas baking is done in the late afternoon/evening (I'm not an early riser!). It is important with gingerbread, as well as shortbread, that the kitchen is cool, and so are your hands, otherwise, you won't get the best results. Once the dough is made, you can always pop it into the fridge for 30 minutes to rest and chill.

This recipe has taken quite a bit of research to get "just right". I wanted a gluten-free gingerbread that held its shape, didn't get the "barking" on the top and had the texture of one with wheat. It took a lot of trial and error, but I guarantee that no one will realise you have made gluten-free with this one.

For the best results, I recommend using the individual flours listed below, but of course, you could use a commercially obtained plain flour blend (all-purpose flour) (1½ cups). As these blends all differ widely, I cannot guarantee the results.

Here are a few tips I discovered during my research:

- Roll the dough to about 5 mm. It will still rise to a nice thickness, but will all cook through and not leave you with a "bendy" biscuit.

You can keep rolling out the dough to use all the scraps, but you may need to chill the dough as working it too much can make it sticky and hard to work with.

- Get good quality cutters. A crisp shape will give you the best results.
- Once the biscuits are cooled, use a pastry brush to brush away any excess flour left by the cutters.
- Make sure to cut the baking paper (parchment) to fit the tray, as the biscuit can become misshapen if the paper is pressing on it.
- Warm icing mix before application, it's a lot easier.

These are perfect for gifts and keep well for 2 weeks in an airtight container (if they don't get eaten first!)

- 75 g brown sugar
- 70 g unsalted butter, at room temperature
- 1 egg
- 65 g white rice flour
- 65 g brown rice flour
- 32 g tapioca flour
- 40 g potato flour
- 35 g cornflour
- 7 g xanthan gum
- ¾ tsp baking soda
- 1¼ tsp ground cinnamon
- 1 tsp ground ginger
- ¼ tsp ground cloves
- ¼ tsp salt
- 3 tbl treacle
- ½ tsp vanilla extract

- Royal icing for decoration (optional)

Preheat oven to 160°C fan/180°C.

Cream butter and sugar until light and fluffy. Add the egg and beat until well combined.

In a separate bowl, whisk together all the dry ingredients. Add these to the butter mixture and mix until well combined. Add the treacle and vanilla and mix well. Turn the mixture onto a floured board and knead lightly until smooth. Place the mixture onto cling wrap, and refrigerate for 30 minutes.

Meanwhile, line 2 baking tins with baking paper.

Remove dough from the fridge, and sandwiched between two sheets of baking paper, roll out to a thickness of 5 mm. Using a cutter dipped in flour, cut out desired shapes and gently place onto the prepared baking tins, leaving about 2-3 cm between each biscuit. Continue until all the dough is used. Place the baking tins in the middle of the oven and bake for 12-15 minutes.

Allow to cool on the baking tins until placing on a wire rack. Decorate with royal icing.

https://youtu.be/2mOubxwupbA

Lemon tart

Makes 8

It's challenging to resist a lemon tart - the crispness of the pastry combined with the tang and smoothness of the filling make this a real winner! However, there are countless horror stories told by home cooks concerning the making of this French classic. About 20 years ago, I experienced one of those moments myself while using standard shortcrust pastry. I had promised to make a lemon tart for my mother-in-law's birthday celebrations. Having followed the recipe, I popped the tart into the oven and settled down for a relaxing cup of tea. Then I began to smell something burning. To my horror, a thick, sticky, yellow ooze was leaking from my wall oven and trickling down the cupboards. Closer inspection of the oven revealed a substantial layer of caramelising lemon custard in the bottom and nearly none left in the now-charred pastry case. What had gone wrong?

The initial problem lay with the pastry case. It's crucial to ensure there are no cracks in the case. To facilitate this, gently use a small ball of the pastry to ease the pastry into the bottom of the tin. This prevents you from accidentally tearing the pastry with your fingertips. Should you notice fine cracks in the pastry shell after baking it, brush a little egg white over the area and "glue" a thin piece of pastry over the crack. This effectively halts any leaks.

Blind baking the crust guarantees a crisp tart shell. To quote Mary Berry from the Great British Bake Off, "Nobody likes a soggy bottom!". To blind bake, you will require a method to weigh down the pastry base. If you don't have ceramic beads, dried chickpeas or uncooked rice will do the job just as well. Another key step is to chill the pastry tin before you blind bake it. This helps to prevent shrinkage and ensures that your filling won't overflow the top of the tin. You can trim the pastry before starting the blind bake if you wish. I prefer to leave the rustic edges, allowing a little room for shrinkage.

Shortcrust Pastry:
- 180 g unsalted butter, cut into cubes
- 240 g plain flour (GF)
- 125 ml cold water

Filling:
- 6 eggs
- 250 g caster sugar
- Grated zest and juice of 3 lemons
- 200 ml cream

Pastry:

Place flour and butter into food processor and pulse until butter is only in small chunks throughout the flour.
Slowly add the water until the pastry forms a ball.

Place on a pastry sheet and knead gently till smooth. Press into a flat cake, wrap in plastic film and place in the fridge for 30 minutes.

Preheat oven to 200°C fan/220°C.

Roll out pastry to fit your tin(s) leaving a little overhang on the edges. Use a ball of trimmings to push the pastry into the sides of the tin. Refrigerate for 30 minutes.

Blind bake for 15 minutes (large tin) or 10 minutes (individual tins).

Remove blind baking beads and then bake for another 5 minutes.

Note if you have any fine cracks - Patch with thin pieces of pastry trimmings, and then brush with egg wash to seal, then place back into the oven for a further 5 minutes.

Allow the cases to cool.
Turn oven down to 160°C fan/180°C.

Filling:

Combine eggs and sugar until well combined. Add juice and stir well. Strain.

Add zest and cream and mix well.

Half fill with filling, then place on the oven rack before fully filling. This eliminates spills getting it into the oven.

Bake for 45 minutes (large) or 30 minutes (individuals). Cook till set but with a slight wobble.

Let it cool in the tin for at least 30 minutes.

Serve dusted with icing sugar and some whipped cream.

Gluten free madeleines

Makes 12

The madeleine is a traditional small cake from the Lorraine region in north-eastern France. It is light, dainty and delicious! Madeleine refers to the distinctive tin that produces shell-shaped cakes.

It has always been my "quick I need to whip up something because guests have just phoned - they are on their way!" dish - that is until recently when I attended a workshop by Petite Cherie. She showed us the technique of resting the batter for at least 2 hours. Although this was for "ordinary" madeleines, not the gluten-free variety that I would be baking.

So off to the test kitchen I headed. I made 2 batches, one that I rested for 2 hours in the fridge, and then just before it was time to put in the oven, I made a second batch - how I was accustomed to. They both went into the oven together, and then we could see the difference. I also used both metal and silicone trays for each batch.

The results: the rested batter was much thicker and harder to pipe into the madeleine tin. It rose slightly more than the other batter and the resulting cakes were much lighter in texture.

- 80 g unsalted butter, melted
- 2 eggs, at room temperature
- 120 g caster sugar
- 30 ml milk, at room temperature
- 165 g plain flour (GF)
- 5 g baking powder (GF)
- Zest of 1 lemon

Preheat oven to 200°C fan/220°C.

Whisk together eggs and sugar until thick. Add milk and mix well.

Combine flour, zest and baking powder. Mix well.

Sprinkle flour mix onto egg mixture and mix well.

Add melted butter and fold through.

Rest mixture in the fridge for 2 hours.

Transfer batter into a piping bag. Fill greased moulds to ¾ full.

Bake for 4 minutes, then reduce heat to 180°C fan/200°C and bake for a further 4 minutes.

Allow to cool in the tray before turning out onto a wire rack.

https://youtu.be/-hH0ivOYMVQ

Gluten free profiteroles

Makes 16

During my trip to France in 2014, it was challenging to watch my partner Myles taste test the delicious French pastries and cakes. Sometimes being coeliac really sucks!

On our first day in Paris, we headed out to a café I had read an article about (which sadly now is no longer in business). It was 10 metro stops from our hotel, but so worth the trek. As I stood there looking at the large display cabinet, filled with so many wonderful treats, I started to cry. The wonderful shop assistant leaned over the counter and handed me a box of tissues, "Don't worry, it happens all the time". Once I had pulled myself together, I was able to choose a delicious éclair filled with a chocolate custard. It was perfect with an espresso, and I cried again!

I have been determined to make these work since my return. And I'm pretty sure I have perfected the choux pastry.

There are some limitations with the gluten-free version. They need to be eaten on the day you make them. They just don't keep. However, I have successfully frozen the uncooked shapes, and then cooked them up when guests arrive.

I have now mastered Crème pâtissière, which is a rich, not too sweet custardy filling used in France to fill the éclairs and profiteroles. I have included the recipe here and updated the chocolate icing. This amended chocolate forms a crisp coating without being too thick.

Pastry:
- 60 g unsalted butter
- Pinch of salt
- ¾ cup water
- 125 g plain flour (GF)
- 3 eggs

Chocolate icing:
- 150 g dark chocolate
- 25 g unsalted butter
- 125 ml thickened cream

Crème pâtissière:
- 250 ml milk
- 1 vanilla pod, split
- 50 g caster sugar
- 3 egg yolks
- 10 g plain flour (GF)
- 10 g cornflour

Preheat oven to 180°C fan/200°C.

Combine salt, butter and water in a medium-sized pot. Bring to the boil and remove from heat.

Add all the flour at once, and stir vigorously. Return to a gentle heat, and continue to stir until mixture begins to leave the sides of the pan.

Allow the mixture to cool slightly.

Transfer the mixture to a stand mixer. Add eggs one at a time, beating well between each addition.

Spoon heaped tablespoons or pipe using a wide nozzle, onto paper-lined baking trays.

Bake for 40 minutes until golden on the outside and dry in the centre.

Allow to cool on the tray before cooling on a wire rack.

When cold, fill with crème pâtissière.

Dip the top into the chocolate mixture.

Chocolate icing:

Gently heat cream to 90°C. Pour over chocolate and stir until melted. Add butter and stir until glossy.

Crème pâtissière:

Scrape vanilla seeds into the milk in a small saucepan. Bring milk and vanilla pod to a simmer. Remove from the heat and remove the vanilla pod.

In a small bowl, whisk sugar, egg yolks and flours together.

Pour ⅓ of milk onto the egg mixture and whisk until well combined.

Pour the egg mixture into the saucepan with the remaining milk and continue to whisk over a medium heat.

Cook until thickened. It will go lumpy - just keep whisking and it will go smooth and glossy. Cook for a further 2 minutes then remove from the heat.

Place in a bowl, cover with cling film, such that the film is touching the contents, to prevent a skin forming, and chill in the fridge until required.

https://youtu.be/gTdw7vkPk9k

Rustic berry tart

Serves 6-8

There's nothing quite like the flavour of fresh, in-season berries. Bursting with colour and intense flavour, they require only minimal intervention to give a dish the "Wow" factor. The French understand this concept well, creating subtle desserts and pastries that showcase the natural attributes of the fruit without excessive added sugar. For this recipe, I've used blueberries, blackberries, raspberries, and strawberries because they're currently in season and abundant at my local market. You could choose just one or two of these, or any other berries you have at hand. Fresh is undoubtedly best, but if you're using frozen, thaw them in a single layer in the fridge to avoid damaging them - the cell structure of the berries will have lost some of its integrity and they can easily crush and dissolve into your crème pâtissière.

During my travels in France, I've always envied Myles' visits to the patisseries - sadly, I've found few gluten-free patisseries in rural France. But that hasn't deterred me from attempting to replicate that wow factor at home, using French techniques.

In this recipe, I've used store-bought gluten-free puff pastry sheets. You could just as easily use "ordinary" puff pastry sheets. While the gluten-free versions still offer a nice crunch, they certainly don't rise or "puff" like their gluten-containing counterparts. The details below include instructions to make about ½ cup of crème pâtissière - this is all you need for this tart. The recipe is scalable, so feel free to double or triple it if you're making other tarts or eclairs.

I can't explain the science behind brushing the pastry case base with reduced balsamic vinegar, but I can confirm it works wonders. Even after storing the tart in the fridge for three days, the gluten-free pastry retained its crunch and didn't turn soggy.

- 1 sheet of ready-rolled puff pastry (GF)
- 1 egg yolk
- 1 tbl water
- 50 ml balsamic vinegar
- 1 tsp lime zest
- 1 tbl lime juice
- ½ cup crème pâtissière
- 250 g mixed fresh berries (strawberries, raspberries, blackberries, blueberries)
- 90 g raspberry jam

Crème Pâtissière:
- 100 ml full cream milk
- ½ vanilla pod
- 20 g caster sugar
- 1 egg yolk
- 10 g cornflour
- ¼ tsp butter

In a small bowl, beat the egg yolk and water.

Roll out the pastry on a lightly floured surface, and cut out a 30 cm x 15 cm rectangle. Carefully roll it onto the rolling pin and transfer to a baking tray lined with baking paper. Brush the edges with the egg yolk mixture. From the leftover pastry, cut two strips 1.5 cm x 30 cm and two strips 1.5 cm x 15 cm. Place these around the edge to form a border and brush with more egg yolk mixture. Prick the base all over with a fork. Cover and chill for 30 minutes.

Meanwhile, place the milk in a small saucepan. Scrape in the vanilla seeds and add the pod. Gently heat until almost simmering, then remove from heat and let cool for 20 minutes.

Whisk the egg yolk and sugar until pale and creamy. Gradually whisk in the cornflour to avoid lumps. Remove the vanilla pod from the milk. Slowly add half the milk to the egg mixture, beat well, then return everything to the pan. Cook over low heat, stirring constantly, until thickened. Remove from heat and stir until smooth. Place the crème pâtissière in a bowl and rub the surface with butter to prevent a skin forming.

Preheat oven to 160°C fan/180°C.

Wash all berries; hull and halve the strawberries.

Bake the pastry case for 20 minutes or until lightly golden. Cool on a wire rack.

Heat the balsamic vinegar in a small pan until reduced by half. Brush the tart base with the reduction. Stir the lime zest and 1 tsp of juice into the crème pâtissière. Spread evenly over the tart base and arrange the fruit on top.

Warm the raspberry jam. If desired, push through a sieve to remove seeds, then brush over the fruit to glaze. Sprinkle over the remaining lime juice and leave to set for at least 30 minutes in a cool place.

https://youtu.be/jfLxWPFvp1E

Traditional shortbread

Makes 24

The days are getting longer and warmer. The fruit trees are in full flower, and my tomato plants are in! That means one thing: Christmas is around the corner!

Christmas is traditionally a time to catch up with friends and relatives and celebrate the year that was. For me, in addition to the usual social gatherings, I also do a lot of cooking for the Country Women's Association of Victoria's Christmas Fare, which is held on the first Saturday of December every year. One of the fastest sellers is shortbread.

Shortbread can be enjoyed all year round, but it has somehow become synonymous with Christmas celebrations. The red Scottish-themed tins full of shortbread are already in stores. But nothing beats homemade!

I have been making shortbread for the family and as gifts since I was in primary school. It is an easy recipe to master, with simple techniques so that kids can help out.

I vividly remember the day I learned this recipe. My mum and I went into town (Melbourne) for the day. It was a rare special treat as Mum had taken the day off work, most likely during school holidays, as workplaces weren't particularly 'family friendly' then. On this trip, we ventured into the Gas and Fuel buildings on Flinders Street. In the 'cooking appliance showroom' we watched cooking demonstrations. I was very excited to be presented with my own copy of "Easy Entertaining with High-Speed Gas". This well-loved, butter-spattered book still gets pulled out each year to prepare this perennial family Christmas favourite recipe. It works especially well gluten-free.

There are endless variations that you can experiment with. I love to add 1½ teaspoons of ground lemon myrtle with the flour to add a very Australian flavour. Ground cardamom, lemon, or orange zest are also great variations.

You can also use stamps, like the ones pictured below, to add patterns to your shortbread. To get the best out of your stamps, roll a walnut-sized piece of dough into a ball. Dip the stamp in caster sugar and gently press down. Place the tray of stamped shortbread into the fridge for 10 minutes before baking to help maintain the pattern on the biscuits.

- 250 g butter, softened
- ½ cup caster sugar
- 2⅔ cups plain flour

Preheat oven to 150°C fan/160°C.

Cream butter and sugar until light and fluffy.

Gradually work in flour, then knead until smooth.

Divide the dough in half.

Press half of the dough into rounds of 20 cm diameter onto baking trays. Use the heel of your hand to spread the dough out until smooth. Level the surface with a spatula, and crimp the edges. Prick the surface with a fork and gently score, halfway through the thickness of the dough, to divide the circle into segments. These are often called petticoats. Repeat with remaining dough.

Alternatively, roll the dough to about 3 cm thick. The dough can then be cut using Christmas biscuit cutters, such as stars or bells. I avoid cutters with fine points, such as Christmas trees, as the dough tends to stick.

Bake in the lower half of the oven for 35-45 minutes.

Keep in an airtight container.

NB - If using gluten-free flour, as always, cool on trays until firm before putting on a wire rack. Otherwise, you will come back to a bench full of crumbs and no biscuits. :(

https://youtu.be/c4Tir4HLIJU

Tarte Tatin (French apple tart)

Serves 10

Every now and then, life presents a little gem that nudges you in an unexpected direction. Some of these shifts are subtle, others monumental. This one leans towards the "subtler" end of the spectrum, but nevertheless marks a definite line in the sand.

In 2018, Myles and I had the good fortune of travelling from San Sebastian (Spain) to Saint Jean Pied de Port (France) in our little hire car. We stopped at the seaside town of Saint Jean de Luz for a stretch and wander. During our stroll through the streets, we came upon a humble A-frame sign declaring "Plats du jour - Confit de canard" and an arrow pointing up a small street. Never ones to pass up a chance to dine on duck, we followed the arrow up the slight incline. What we found was a charming little café, seating probably only 20 or so patrons. Each table was dressed with red checked tablecloths, including the large communal table, which had two spare seats. Along one wall, a table groaned under an assortment of incredible-looking desserts, including an eye-catching Tarte Tatin (apple tart). The lunch was a two-course affair, and naturally, we both opted for Confit du canard, served with the crispest lettuce and hand-cut chips. Absolute perfection on a plate!

Myles had set his sights on the apple tart. We had started to chat with the gentleman sitting next to us and his son. His English was flawless - he was Swiss and owned a holiday house in the town. He dined here every day for lunch. In fact, we were probably the only non-locals in the cafe. Much to Myles' disappointment, it was explained that Chef Michel only made one Tarte Tatin a day - the locals didn't ring up to reserve a table, but they did ring to reserve a slice of that tart! Myles missed out, but was thoroughly satisfied with the berry compote he had instead. My rice cream was absolutely sublime.

This experience set us on a quest for the perfect Tarte Tatin. I'm not sure if Myles will ever stop ruing the missed chance to taste Chef Michel's tart, but the journey has undeniably been delectable.

The history of this dish is rather fascinating. It was originally created by two sisters who ran the Hôtel Tatin in Lamotte-Beuvron, Loir-et-Cher in the 1880s. The story of its origin has several variations, but all agree it was an accidental creation that proved immensely popular with guests.

To make a successful Tatin, you need a dish that can go from stovetop to oven. A dish with sloping sides is advantageous for easy turning out, but it's not strictly necessary.

There's debate over whether puff or shortcrust was the original pastry used. I prefer shortcrust to balance out the dish, but you can certainly use either.

I've used Granny Smith apples as they hold their shape well. Originally, the sisters used Reine des Reinetes Pippins and Calvilles. Golden Delicious or Gala apples would also work well. Opt for small apples as they create a better design and fit more snugly when the tart is turned out. Other fruits such as pears, quinces or peaches can also be used.

The tart should be served lukewarm. Traditionally, it's not served with cream or ice cream; one simply savours the sweet caramel of the dish on its own.

- 200 g sweet shortcrust pastry
- 90 g butter
- 250 g white sugar
- 1 kg apples (Granny Smiths)
- Juice of ½ lemon

Roll pastry to 3 mm thick and cut to 5 mm larger than your tin.

Prick pastry with a fork and place into the fridge to rest.

Preheat oven to 210°C fan/230°C

Peel apples, cut into ¼ and remove cores.

Melt butter in the tin, then add sugar and stir until a caramel forms.

Place the apples close together into the tin and baste with lemon juice. Cook for 10 minutes.

Remove pan from heat and carefully cover apples with pastry tucking the pastry into the dish.

Bake in the oven for 15 minutes until pastry is golden.

Allow the dish to cool on a cake rack for 20-25 minutes.

Carefully turn out the tart onto a serving plate.

Serve lukewarm.

https://youtu.be/n6hgzIV5-K8

Raspberry macarons with dark chocolate ganache

Makes 24

When I go to a café with friends, I often pick a macaron — something I never make at home. Naturally gluten-free and full of vibrant colours and flavours, they're perfect with a short black.

Macarons became hugely popular in Australia in the 2000s, thanks to a MasterChef contestant whose signature dish was macarons. He went on to open patisseries and host dessert shows. I used to think they were hard to make — contestants always looked stressed.

Then in 2023, while in Paris, I took a class where we made chocolate and pistachio macarons. With a few tricks, I discovered they're surprisingly doable, and perfect for experimenting.

You don't need fancy trays — just a flat baking tray, baking paper (or Silpat), and a piping bag with a plain nozzle (I use size 12). Good piping technique helps get even shells.

A great tip I learned: age your egg whites. Separate and leave them uncovered in the fridge for 1–2 days. This reduces moisture and helps form a stable meringue. Weigh the egg whites — this sets the amounts of sugar and almond flour. If you're using liquid colouring or flavouring, add it with the white sugar so it blends well.

Almond flour is not almond meal — it's finer and made from blanched almonds, not whole ones.

The key technique is macaronage: folding the batter until it's smooth and slowly flowing. Humidity, food colouring, and meringue texture all affect how long this takes. The batter should fall slowly from the spatula, forming figure 8s without breaking. If it runs quickly, it's been overmixed or the meringue was too soft.

You can let the batter rest for 30 minutes before piping, but I usually pipe right away. Once piped, bang the tray on the bench to release air bubbles. Let it sit until the surface is dry to the touch — around 40 minutes. Add any toppings at this point. This drying step helps the shells form their signature "foot" — a good sign you nailed the texture.

The teacher told us unfilled shells freeze well, though I've yet to try — we ate ours too fast! You can be endlessly creative with colours and flavours. I've swapped in freeze-dried black cherries for raspberries to make a black forest version. Bon appétit!

- 100 g egg white, room temp
- 100 g white sugar
- 100 g almond flour
- 100 g icing sugar
- 20 g freeze-dried raspberry powder
- 10 g freeze-dried raspberry pieces (optional)

Ganache:
- 100 g dark chocolate, broken into small pieces
- 40 g salted butter, room temperature
- 60 g cream

Place egg whites in a large bowl and whisk on medium speed until fluffy. Add white sugar in three batches, whisking until combined. Increase to high speed and whisk until stiff peaks form.

Sift together almond flour, icing sugar, and raspberry powder. Add to the meringue and mix on low speed with a flat beater for 10 seconds, then on medium for another 10 seconds. Check for macaronage — the batter should form a ribbon when dropped from a spoon. If not ready, gently fold by hand until achieved. Don't overmix!

Line trays with baking paper. Using a piping bag with a small round nozzle, pipe an even number (about the size of a 20-cent coin), spacing slightly. Sprinkle raspberry pieces on half. Tap trays on the bench to remove air bubbles. Let sit at room temperature for 30–45 minutes, until the tops are no longer tacky to the touch.

Preheat oven to 145°C fan/165°C.

Bake on the lower rack for 15 minutes (17 minutes if using Silpat). Cool completely before removing from the tray.

To make the ganache:

Heat cream until just boiling. Place butter and chocolate in a bowl. Pour hot cream over and stir until smooth. The ganache will thicken as it cools.

To assemble:

Match biscuit halves by size. Pipe ganache onto one shell, avoiding the edges. Top with a second shell and twist gently to spread the filling evenly.

Crème caramel

Serves 6

Next to fruit salad, crème caramel is possibly the most common gluten-free dessert served to coeliacs at catered functions or on many restaurant menus. I am not sure why, but I had always assumed it was a difficult dish to make. I think it's because I didn't understand the chemistry that turns the hard caramel into the sweet and plentiful sauce that crowns the silky smooth custard. Doing the research for this recipe, I discovered that the secret is actually as simple as time. Sugar is hydrophilic—meaning it absorbs moisture, in this case from the custard. Somewhat surprisingly, the longer you keep the cooked crème caramels in the fridge, the more sauce you get. Serving them on the day you make them leaves most of the caramel hard in the bottom of the ramekin dish. By day 2 or 3, the majority of sugar has softened into the sauce.

It is important to gently bake the custards to get the silky smooth texture without the custard curdling or forming a hard crust before the middle is cooked. The humidity from the steam that rises as the water heats helps keep the top of the custard from becoming too dry. An easy bain marie is to use a tea towel to line a baking dish, which is then filled with hot water up to halfway up the sides of the ramekins. The tea towel also acts as a barrier between the ramekin and the baking dish. This stops the bottom of the ramekin from getting too hot and the custard cooking unevenly. Your tea towel won't burn, it will just get wet :)

To make this restaurant-quality dish, making them a day or 2 before you want to serve them gives the best results. Possibly the "scariest part" is decanting the dessert from the ramekin onto the plate. You will need to gently loosen the top of the baked custard from the sides of the dish. I also found that once inverted on the plate, a sudden movement side to side allows you to feel the dessert shift in the ramekin, releasing the suction. Then as you lift the ramekin, the custard is settled nicely on your serving plate and the sauce cascades down onto the plate.

Caramel:
- 200 g caster sugar
- ½ cup water

Custard:
- 100 g caster sugar
- 300 ml cream
- 1½ cups milk
- 4 eggs
- 2 egg yolks
- 1 vanilla pod

Preheat the oven to 150°C fan/170°C.

To make the caramel:

Combine 200 g caster sugar with ½ cup water over low heat, stirring until dissolved. Increase heat and bring to a boil, brushing down the sides of the pot to prevent sugar crystals from sticking. Boil until a deep caramel/mahogany colour (5-7 minutes).

Remove from heat and allow bubbles to subside. Pour into 6 straight-sided 1-cup ramekins, turning carefully to coat the sides. Chill until the caramel has set (20 minutes in the fridge).

To make the custard:

Combine cream, milk, and split vanilla pod in a medium saucepan. Heat over moderate heat for 6 minutes until small bubbles begin to appear on the side of the pan, stirring occasionally.

In a bowl, gently whisk eggs, egg yolks, and remaining sugar using a fork. You don't want to create a foam. Pour in milk slowly and combine. Strain the egg mixture and then pour into prepared ramekins.

Place ramekins in a tea towel-lined baking dish and pour in hot water until just over halfway up the sides of the ramekins.

Bake for 35-40 minutes until just set. Remove from the baking dish and allow to cool on a wire rack until it reaches room temperature. Refrigerate overnight.

To serve, allow ramekin to come to room temperature. Invert onto a deep plate and swish to the side to release the custard. Gently remove the ramekin. The custard should be surrounded by the dark caramel sauce as it cascades down the sides.

https://youtu.be/ydld-NTpuI4

Beef burgundy

Serves 4

When it's cold and wet outside, nothing beats a hearty casserole or stew to warm you through. This dish, based on the French classic, is a family favourite. It can be cooked in the oven or on the stove top. The long cooking time means that cheaper cuts of meat are ideal for this dish, as cooking on a low heat for an extended period in liquid encourages the breakdown of connective tissues, including the protein collagen, which renders the meat tough when cooked rapidly. Since the cheaper cuts of beef can be fattier, this also helps to ensure the beef doesn't dry out, whilst adding extra flavour. However, don't skimp on the wine - if it's not good enough to drink, it's not good enough to cook with!

Be careful when seasoning this dish. The pancetta will naturally add salt, so there's no need to add much. A common mistake is to sprinkle pepper as if seasoning your own plate - remember, this dish serves four. The choice between freshly ground and pre-ground pepper will make a noticeable difference. You can always add more, but it's difficult to rectify if you've added too much.

The resulting sauce from this recipe should be silky. If the sauce is too dry, it indicates that you have simmered too vigorously. Gentle cooking is definitely the key.

- 750 g diced beef (chuck steak or topside)
- 12 pickling onions, peeled and left whole
- 200 g button mushrooms, halved
- 100 g pancetta/bacon, diced
- 3 cloves garlic, crushed
- 1 tbl plain flour
- 1 bouquet garni (2 bay leaves, 3 sprigs parsley, 1 sprig thyme tied with kitchen string)
- 2 cups beef stock
- 2 cups red wine
- Olive oil
- Salt and pepper, to taste

In a heavy-based pot, heat a little olive oil. Sear the beef well - approximately 10 minutes.

Add flour and cook for 2 minutes.

Add stock and wine deglazing the pan. Bring the pot to the boil.

Add bouquet garni and turn down to a simmer. Add the garlic.

In a separate pan with a little olive oil, caramelize the onions till golden. Add onions to meat and simmer 45 minutes.

In a separate pan, fry pancetta until crispy. Add in the mushrooms and fry for 2-3 minutes. Add to the meat. Taste for seasoning adding salt and pepper if required. Simmer gently for a further 15 minutes. Remove bouquet garni and discard.

Serve with creamy mashed potato or polenta.

https://youtu.be/KggZbf_zA1g

Cornish pasties

Makes 8-10

There is a lot of tradition surrounding pasties. My mum's family, the Allens, were Cornish miners who emigrated to Australia during the gold rush of the 1850s. They eventually settled in Bendigo, and their mining skills were put to good use. They brought with them many family recipes, and the recipe I am sharing with you today is one of them. I have heard many family debates over whether peas should be included in the recipe. In my household, this was a distinct "no!" but a number of my cousins would vehemently disagree. The choice is yours.

Cornish Pasties have received PGI (Protected Geographical Indication). A PGI is created to protect regional foods that have a specific quality, reputation, or other characteristic attributable to that area. It acts like a trademark and stops manufacturers from outside the region from copying a regional product. However, this doesn't stop us from making them at home.

Cornish pasties have a distinct look - they have the pastry folded at the top, creating a handle. These calorie-filled parcels were taken down into the mines for the miners' meals. Some historians state that the handle could then be thrown away, not contaminating the food with their dirty hands. This is due to the use of arsenic in the tin mines. This does seem wasteful in a time when food was expensive and nothing was wasted.

Making pasties in my house was always an all-in affair. Dad was in charge of rolling out the puff pastry, Mum minced the vegetables and then put the filling onto the circles of pastry, my brother brushed the edges with milk, and I folded them together and pricked the sides once they went on the tray. Then we all waited together for them to come out of the oven, golden brown and tasting amazing!

I am privileged to be the custodian of the cast iron mincer. It has an amazing story that I have shared in my cookbook "Origins".

Below is our family recipe.

- 2 packets of puff pastry sheets (GF)
- 750 g minced meat
- 1 swede (neep)
- 2 potatoes
- 5 carrots
- 1 tbl salt
- Milk
- 1 egg, beaten

Preheat oven to 190°C fan/210°C.

Mince all the vegetables together using a food processor. Mix them with the minced meat and salt.

Stand the bowl at an angle to allow some of the liquid to drain away while you prepare the pastry. If the filling is too moist, the pasties will leak juices and soften the pastry while waiting to go into the oven.

Roll out the puff pastry sheets to approximately 3 mm thickness. Use a bread and butter plate as your template and cut a circle of pastry. Spoon a large spoonful of the mixture onto the middle of the circle.

Using a pastry brush, paint the edges of the circle with milk.

Fold the two halves of the pastry over the filling, gently pressing the edges together. Roll the join to get a good seal, thus making the 'handle' of the pasty and gently twist the ends together.

Continue with the remaining pastry until all the ingredients are used. It is okay to reroll the scraps of pastry from each sheet.

Place the pasties on a lined baking tray.

Using a fork, prick both sides of the pasty to allow air to escape. Brush the pasties with beaten egg.

Place in the oven for 25 minutes until golden brown.

Serve with homemade tomato sauce.

Ham and cheese potato croquettes

Makes 12

In my humble opinion, there's no bad way to serve a potato! Mashed, fried, baked, on a stick, chipped, scalloped... This recipe combines several of the best characteristics of the potato - its creamy smoothness and crunch. Furthermore, it offers cooks endless possibilities based on what's available in the fridge - leftover roast meat, salami, flaked pieces of cooked fish, grated carrot, or finely diced fresh asparagus, just to list a few suggestions.

A number of years ago, while travelling through Spain, I discovered croquetas - crunchy, smooth morsels served at tapas bars at room temperature. Although they look similar to the croquette recipe I'm sharing with you today, there's a significant difference between the Spanish and French recipes - croquetas are made with a thick béchamel that supports the fillings, often jamón or chorizo. This makes a gluten-free option slightly more challenging. The recipe listed below is therefore French-based, using mashed potatoes to support the flavours of the ham and cheese.

Like when making gnocchi, potato croquettes work best when floury potatoes are used. You also want to avoid making the potato "soggy". To do this, the potatoes can be boiled in their skins or steamed. This will give you a better finished texture, and the croquettes won't fall apart. For a great texture, use a mouli or ricer to mash the potatoes. However, if you don't have one, a potato masher will do the job just fine.

Cooked croquettes can also be frozen. I've made a small batch here, but it's easy to scale up, freeze, and then reheat in a moderate oven (190°C) for 20 minutes. These are great to serve with drinks, or as a light meal served with a crisp green salad. They've quickly become one of our family favourites.

- 250 g potatoes
- 75 g ham, finely diced
- ½ cup grated Jarlsberg cheese
- 1 tbl aioli
- 1½ tbl whole egg mayonnaise
- Salt and pepper, to taste
- ½ cup plain flour
- 1 egg
- 1½ cups dried breadcrumbs
- Rice bran or light vegetable oil, for frying

Boil or steam the potatoes in their jackets until tender. Allow to cool slightly, and peel. Mash until smooth.

Add ham, cheese, salt and pepper. Stir well.

Add mayonnaise and aioli and stir until well combined.

Line a baking tray with baking paper. Using heaped dessert spoon, divide the mixture into 12 pieces, placing each on the tray.

Place the flour in a small bowl. In another small bowl beat the egg lightly. Place the breadcrumbs on a plate.

Working one at a time, take a ball of potato mix and form into a small log shape. Place back onto the tray.

Take each croquette and lightly dust in flour, then dip into the egg and then gently roll in the breadcrumbs. Place back onto the tray.

Place the tray of crumbed croquettes in the fridge for 20 minutes. This helps maintain their shape during cooking.

In a heavy based frypan, add oil to approximately 1 cm deep. Gently heat until 170°C. Shallow fry the croquettes until golden all over.

Place on paper towel to drain, before serving.

https://youtu.be/YRwMyPALV60

Traditional seafood paella (Paella de marisco)

Serves 2

Looking back over all the recipes I've made into YouTube videos, I was surprised to realise I've never done Paella — even though I cook it often for guests or just the two of us. It's an easy dish to master, and one that spans from street food to fine dining, depending on the ingredients you use. This recipe serves 2–3 but scales easily.

Paella is made to be shared, and the ingredients can vary depending on preference. I sometimes swap the seafood for diced chorizo and chicken thighs — it depends on who I'm feeding and how I feel :). My Spanish friends despair at the inclusion of chorizo, which isn't traditional, but here in Australia, it's almost expected. Today's version stays true to the traditional style.

The rice — arroz in Spanish — matters. Bomba, Calasparra, or Valencia varieties are best. I usually use Bomba or Calasparra, easily found at local supermarkets or fresh produce markets. Spanish grocers often stock all three. These short-grain types absorb flavour beautifully without going mushy. Arborio can substitute in a pinch, though it goes creamy if stirred too much.

If you don't have a paella pan, a large frypan works fine — just ensure the rice sits 2–3 cm deep for even cooking.

As with all simple dishes, stock quality matters. I use mussel stock saved throughout the year from cooking Portarlington mussels (#MrMussel). Good store-bought chicken stock works too. I personally find commercial fish stock too overpowering — but it's personal preference.

I had the great privilege of learning paella from Candido at Barcelona Cooking (https://www.barcelonacooking.net/en/). I highly recommend their classes if you visit Barcelona. Candido took us through La Boqueria market and taught us to appreciate Spanish ingredients — and how to spot a quality paella. In a restaurant, it should arrive in the pan it was cooked in, with seafood artfully arranged. Most importantly, it should have a crisp golden base, called socarrat — my favourite part! Street paella, made in huge pans serving 50+, these are unlikely to have socarrat, but are still delicious.

- 180 g rice (Bomba, Calasparra or Valencia varieties are best)
- 6 mussels
- 4 green prawns in shell
- 1 squid hood or 125 g cuttlefish
- 100 g firm white fish fillet
- 1 onion, finely chopped
- 1 clove garlic, crushed
- 2 ripe tomatoes
- 6 saffron threads
- ¼ tsp pimento or paprika (omit if adding chorizo)
- 500 ml fish or chicken stock
- 3 tbl olive oil
- 100 g frozen peas
- Salt to taste
- Lemon and chopped parsley to serve

Place the mussels in a small bowl with clean cold water.

Dice the squid into small squares approx 1 cm x 1 cm. Chop the fish into bite-sized pieces.

Cut the tomatoes in half and grate - discarding the skin.

In a paella pan, heat the oil. Sauté the prawns for 1 minute on each side until they turn pink. Remove the prawns from the pan and set aside until they are needed later.

In the same oil, sauté the squid and onion gently. As the onion becomes golden, add the peas and cook for another 2 minutes. Now add the tomato pulp and garlic. Gently sauté until the juice from the tomato has evaporated, and the onions have caramelised.

In a small pot, heat the fish stock until it is simmering. Add the saffron to the stock.

Add the rice, pimento and fish pieces to the paella pan and gently stir for 1 minute, coating the rice with the tomato oil. Add all the stock at once and stir to combine. Turn the heat to high, and allow to cook for 5 minutes.

Debeard the mussels and place mussels around the pan, pushed slightly into the rice. Turn the heat to low and cook for another 10 minutes. Return the prawns to the top of the dish, and cook for another 3-5 minutes.

Paella should stand for 3-5 minutes before serving. There should be a crust formed at the bottom of the pan (it's the best bit!). Serve with a wedge of lemon, a sprinkle of chopped parsley and a crisp Rosé.

Mussels with tomato and chorizo

Serves 2-3

I volunteer at the Portarlington Mussel Festival every January. For the past few years, I've hosted cooking demos on stage — showing how to easily de-beard mussels, cook them perfectly, and, importantly, how to spot the ones you shouldn't cook. So it's time to share some of these tips with you!

First — if you can, buy mussels direct from the farmer. Like most farmers, they're full of great advice and recipe suggestions. I'm lucky to live just 1.5 hours from Portarlington, where many of Victoria's mussels are farmed. Jennifer from Mr Mussel has taught me heaps — including how to tell boy mussels from girl mussels (you'll have to watch my YouTube video to find out how!).

Second — storage. Mussels need to stay cold and damp. The best way is in a bowl or foam container in the fridge, covered with a damp tea towel. They'll stay fresh for up to 7 days. Alternatively, you can cook and freeze them (out of the shell) for up to 2 months.

Third — how do you know if a mussel is bad? Many people say, "If it doesn't open when cooked." That's a myth! You need to test mussels before cooking — once they're in the pot, they're already dead!

Here's what to check:

* Broken shell? Toss it.

* Shell open in the fridge? Tap it on the bench. If it slowly closes, it's alive and safe to cook. No movement? Discard it.

And those mussels that stay closed during cooking? They're often the biggest and juiciest. They may have started to open, then clamped shut. They're safe to eat — just be careful, they can hold very hot liquid inside.

This recipe is a crowd favourite and scales up beautifully for family or friends.

- 2 dozen fresh mussels (approx. 700 g)
- 6 button mushrooms, sliced
- 1 red onion, finely diced
- 150 g speck/pancetta, cut into batons
- 1 chorizo, finely diced
- 750 ml passata/sugo
- Parsley, chopped for garnish

Pasta to serve.

Place mussels in a large bowl of tap water and allow to sit for at least 10 minutes. This allows the mussels to open and release some of the salt water and grit inside their shells.

Strain mussels and place in a large pan. Cover with a lid and cook on medium heat. When the pan is foaming (like a bad Cappuccino), the mussels will have opened. Using tongs, remove opened mussels and place in a bowl. See note below on how to open the closed mussels. When cool enough to handle, de-beard the mussels. Strain the liquid in the pan - this can be used as stock for risottos, soups, paella, etc.

In a large saucepan, gently fry the speck and chorizo until starting to brown. Add the mushrooms and onion and cook for 3 minutes. Add the passata and stir well.

Meanwhile, cook your pasta.

Once the pasta is cooked, return mussels to the sauce and stir through to warm them. Serve on a bed of pasta, garnished with parsley.

Note:

Squeeze the sides of the mussel. The top will open slightly and you will be able to get the point of a knife into the shell. Wiggle the knife down until you feel the join of the mussel. Push through and the mussel will open. Be CAREFUL, the mussel is likely to be full of hot liquid.

* Do not cook a mussel that has a broken shell or that remains open when you take it from the rinse water and after you have tapped it on the bench. These are dead and therefore not fresh and should be disposed of.

https://youtu.be/517r8WDJ060

Potato rösti

Makes 12

Potatoes have to be my favorite vegetable. There is no bad way to eat them—roasted, mashed, fried... Among all of these methods, those with "crunchy bits" are particularly delicious. Therefore, Potato Rösti hits the mark as a standout choice. The grated potatoes offer numerous crispy bits, and when paired with something soft and creamy, the combination is simply perfect.

Many cultures feature a version of rösti. It's a traditional dish of Switzerland. A quick search on the internet reveals a variety of methods, some of which include egg and flour. These, however, can be problematic for those with coeliac disease due to the use of gluten-rich flour.

This recipe contains no flour, so it poses no issues for those avoiding gluten. The röstis hold together well, have just the right amount of crunch, and are quick to prepare — perfect for brunch or a light meal.

The only drawback is that you need to prepare and eat them immediately. They aren't suitable to prepare the night before or to reheat.

You can use any waxy potato. For a twist, try using 1 kg of potatoes and 1 kg of sweet potatoes. Consider adding fresh herbs, bacon batons, or grated zucchini (courgette).

I often serve these röstis with a poached egg for brunch or with smoked salmon, avocado, and crème fraîche for a lighter meal. However you prefer them, they're quick and easy to prepare.

- 2 kg potatoes, peeled
- 1 large brown onion
- 60 g butter, melted
- Salt and pepper, to taste
- Vegetable oil, for frying

- 1 avocado
- 125 g crème fraîche
- 300 g smoked salmon

Grate the onion and potato coarsely.

Place the vegetables in a colander. Using your hands, squeeze out as much of the liquid as you can.

Transfer to a bowl and add the melted butter, salt and pepper. Mix until well combined.

Add oil in a heavy based frypan to a depth of 1 cm. When it reaches 200°C spoon approximately ⅓ cup of the mixture into the pan. Flatten the rösti using an egg slide. Only cook 2 rösti at a time, so as to not crowd the pan. Cook 3-4 minutes on each side.

Transfer cooked rösti to a tray lined with paper towel to absorb the oil. Repeat with remaining batter.

Serve immediately with slices of avocado, a spoon of creme fresh and a piece of smoked salmon. per rosti. Sprinkle with chopped fresh chives or a sprig of dill.

https://youtu.be/BEH6y0mgsQM

Celeriac and potato dauphinoise

Serves 4

Potatoes are my favourite vegetable! I don't think you can serve them in a way that isn't delicious and filling. A particularly decadent way of serving them is in a bubbling creamy sauce. The French, of course, developed more than one way to serve bubbling creamy potatoes - gratin and dauphinoise. Potatoes au gratin are slices of pre-cooked (usually boiled) potatoes cooked in cream with added flour and topped with cheese in a shallow baking dish. Dauphinoise, on the other hand, is a dish made of thinly-sliced (not pre-cooked) potatoes that cook in cream and baked at a lower temperature so that the potatoes cook through without becoming too crunchy on top. Dauphinoise are usually cooked in deep baking dishes. These differ from scalloped potatoes, which are made with a flour-butter-milk roux.

When choosing potatoes, floury varieties such as Coliban, King Edward, Sebago, or Golden Delight are ideal. In Australia, the most common starchy potato is Sebago (those dirt-brushed potatoes), Dutch creams, or Red Delight. In America – the Russet variety and for those of you in Europe, King Edward or Maris Piper are perfect. These potatoes are high in starch and low in moisture, resulting in dry, flaky flesh that breaks down and fluffs up when cooked, absorbing other liquids and flavours—particularly milk and butter. If you use waxy potatoes, the layers slip and slide when serving.

Celeriac is not a vegetable that I grew up with. It is very versatile and can be eaten raw (e.g., in celeriac remoulade) or it can be cooked. It is quite sweet with a subtle celery flavour and lower in carbohydrates than potatoes. It is in season from May to August in the Southern Hemisphere or September to April in the Northern Hemisphere. It has plenty of health benefits including being a source of vitamins B6, C, and K, fibre, antioxidants, and minerals. I often boil it in milk and mash it, serving as an alternative to mashed potatoes.

Combining these two vegetables lightens this dish a little without removing its decadence. The choice of cheese will change the flavour of this dish. Gruyère is the best as it provides flavour and browns beautifully on top. It's quite expensive so for everyday purposes, you can substitute Colby, Cheddar, Havarti, or Tasty cheese.

This dish can be reheated the next day, allowing the flavours to further develop. Perfect for lunch with a crisp green salad, or as an accompaniment with roasted meats.

- 1 medium celeriac (approx. 400 g)
- 500 g potatoes, floury variety recommended (e.g., Coliban, King Edward, Sebago, Golden Delight)
- 200 ml cream
- 200 ml milk
- 2 cloves garlic
- 2 tsp freshly grated nutmeg
- Salt and pepper to taste
- 1 tbl fresh thyme (optional)
- 100 g Gruyère cheese, grated
- Knob of butter

Preheat oven to 160°C fan/180°C.

First, slice your celeriac and potatoes into thin slices.

Place the slices of celeriac and potatoes in a large saucepan and add the garlic, cream, milk, and nutmeg. (It won't cover the vegetables). Cover with a lid and bring to a simmer on medium heat and cook gently for 5 minutes. Add thyme if using.

Remove from the heat and allow to cool slightly.

Grease a baking dish with the butter. Using a slotted spoon, lift out the vegetables and arrange them in the baking dish in flat layers. Press down to create a firmly packed and even layer. Season with salt and pepper between layers. Pour the creamy liquid over the top and gently shake the dish to distribute the liquid and ensure an even layer in the dish. Scatter over the Gruyère cheese.

Bake for 45 minutes until the top bubbles and turns golden brown. Let stand for 15 minutes before serving.

Serve with roast meat or a side salad for a light lunch.

https://youtu.be/308j2QRZjIE

Roast duck with cherry sauce

Serves 2

It is not uncommon to hear friends and acquaintances say they love eating duck, but never cook it at home. After our first trip to France in 2015, my fear of cooking duck has dissipated. Before venturing to the Dordogne, I had never cooked duck - yet always ordered it when eating out. I, like my friends, had something in my head that suggested duck was difficult to perfect. How wrong was I!

Duck needs care. Always pat the duck dry with paper towels. This leads to crispier skin. If you are using duck breast, score the skin in a diamond pattern just through the fat and not into the meat. This allows the fat to render - giving a perfect crispness to the skin, but also giving you duck fat to cook the best roast potatoes ever! Always salt the duck prior to cooking.

For best results, allow the meat to come to room temperature before cooking. This way you have greater control over the temperature of the meat. This ensures you don't overcook and dry out your duck pieces.

Remember not to throw away your rendered duck fat either. Place it in a sealed container and store it in the fridge for next time you are roasting potatoes.

The second series of YouTube videos will be focusing on some of the cooking challenges, and what better way to start than with duck? (and it's even naturally gluten-free!)

- 2 duck legs
- 2 baking potatoes
- A few sprigs of fresh thyme
- Sea salt flakes and pepper

Sauce:
- 200 ml port
- 200 ml chicken stock
- A few sprigs of thyme
- 100 g pitted black cherries
- 20 g cold butter, cut into cubes
- 1 tsp cornflour mixed with 1 tbl cold water (optional)
- Salt and pepper to taste

Preheat oven to 200°C fan/220°C.

Sprinkle salt over the skin of the duck. Heat a small frypan and sear the duck legs skin-side down until the skin turns golden and renders out some fat.

Place the legs, skin side up in a small roasting dish.

Cut the potatoes into 2 cm slices across, then cut each slice into 4. Arrange these potato pieces around the duck legs, then let a few sprigs of thyme fall over the duck and potatoes, and season with salt and pepper before putting into the preheated oven.

Cook for 1.5 hours, occasionally turning the potatoes.

With fifteen minutes of cooking time left to go, and using the same frypan that you cooked the duck in, drain off any excess fat and deglaze with port, taking care to stand back as the pan may flame.

Add the cherries, thyme and chicken stock and bring to the boil.

Lower the heat to simmering point and allow the sauce to bubble away until the mixture is reduced by about half.

Add the cold butter and shake the pan until the butter has melted and the sauce has thickened slightly.

If the sauce has not thickened enough pour in the cornflour slurry whilst constantly stirring.

French styled chicken casserole

Serves 2

For many, French cooking conjures images of gastronomy, high-end restaurants, crisp white tablecloths, and exquisitely plated dishes. While it is indeed all of those things, French cuisine also celebrates regional dishes, quality ingredients, classic food pairings, and a mastery of technique.

I've been fortunate enough to explore various regions of France. On each visit, a trip to the local market is a must. The array of fresh produce is astounding—varieties of tomatoes and peaches I'd never seen before, the sweetest strawberries, a wealth of vanilla pods, fresh white asparagus, and cheeses made locally from sheep, cow, and goat milk. It's truly a foodie's paradise.

Though supermarkets are certainly available, the weekly fresh market offers the best snapshot of what's local and in season. It's also an ideal spot to people-watch; you can observe what shoppers are gravitating towards, which bunch of tarragon they pick and which they pass over, and what mix of vegetables they choose. While my French is far from fluent, I can still sense the spirited discussions taking place between shopper and farmer over the quality of the produce.

This dish exemplifies what you often see on the "Plat du jour" chalkboards—simple, quality ingredients in classic combinations that work seamlessly together.

- 2 chicken Marylands, jointed
- 200 g button mushrooms, quartered
- 100 g speck or bacon, sliced
- 10 g butter
- 1 tbl olive oil
- 100 ml Chardonnay
- 1 brown onion, sliced
- 1 bay leaf
- 2 sprigs rosemary
- 2 tbl vegetable oil
- 2 medium potatoes, cubed

Heat oil and butter in a heavy-based casserole dish and brown the chicken pieces.

Season with salt and pepper. Add the onion, speck, rosemary, bay leaf and gently cook for 2-3 minutes.

Add the wine and bring to the boil. Stir in the mushrooms. Cover with foil and a lid and cook over a low heat for 30 minutes.

Meanwhile, heat the vegetable oil in a heavy frypan and cook the potato cubes for about 15 minutes until almost cooked.

Transfer the potatoes to the chicken dish and stir gently. Cook for a further 5 minutes.

Serve with a crisp salad or some steamed green beans and a glass of Chardonnay.

https://youtu.be/l_JgBpc-WnQ

Pulpo con pimentón (Spanish octopus with paprika)

Serves 4-6

I absolutely love eating octopus! Growing up, it wasn't a common food in Australia and was hard to come by. Thankfully, that's changed—you can now find it at most fishmongers. Sometimes, it's baby octopus—perfect grilled and served with crisp lettuce, black Kalamata olives, goat cheese, and a light vinaigrette.

My Maltese relatives often made a mouth-watering octopus stew with rich tomato sauce, potatoes, and capers, all served over spaghetti. Aunty Vivi insisted on tossing a red wine cork into the pot to keep the octopus tender. I never argued—and I've never had tough octopus. That might be because, after a cup of wine went in, the rest of the bottle went to the cook. No cork, no waste! But today, we're doing something different.

In 2017, I spent two amazing days at the MIMO Basque Cooking School in San Sebastian. The tutors chuckled at the cork theory. They explained that plunging the octopus into boiling water helps convert the collagen into silky gelatin. Patience is key during the gentle simmer. And it's much easier to portion once it's cooked.

Freezing also helps tenderise the tentacles—just thaw in the fridge before cooking.

Another key ingredient here is paprika. There are three types: sweet, smoked, and hot. Each has a unique flavour and isn't easily swapped. Sweet paprika adds colour and a sweet pepper flavour. Smoked paprika—dried over oak—adds rich depth. Genuine Spanish pimentón is made using traditional EU-protected methods. Hot paprika is the Hungarian style.

For this dish, I use both sweet and hot smoked paprika to create a distinct, slightly spicy flavour.

In Spain, octopus is often prepared this way and served as pintxos or tapas. Imagine crusty bread with a slice of potato and octopus, drizzled with paprika oil—delicious, though rarely gluten-free. I've served mine with a capsicum emulsion and Spanish sea salt.

Emulsion
- 3 red capsicums
- 1 tbl red wine vinegar
- ½ cup olive oil

Blacken the capsicum skins over an open flame. Place in a plastic bag to sweat. Remove the skins—it's fine if a few flecks remain. Remove seeds. Roughly chop and blend with vinegar to a purée. Slowly add the oil. Season with salt.

- 1 kg adult octopus
- Sea salt
- 5 g sweet paprika
- 5 g hot paprika (pimentón)
- Olive oil

Bring a large pot of water with 2 generous pinches of sea salt to the boil.

Dunk the whole octopus into the water for 5 seconds then remove. Dunk the octopus for a second time for 5 seconds then remove. Dunk the octopus for a third and final time for 5 seconds then remove.

Return the water to a gentle boil. Place the octopus in the water and gently boil for 30 - 40 minutes. Turn off the heat and leave the octopus in the water for another 30 minutes. The top of the legs should be tender when gently squeezed.

Remove the octopus from the water. Remove all the legs from the body. Portion the octopus into serving size pieces. Discard the hood and beak sections.

Mix the two types of paprika with some olive oil.

Heat a little olive oil in a heavy frypan on a low heat and gently fry the octopus for 2 minutes on each side. Brush each piece of octopus with the paprika oil and return to the hot pan. Be careful not to burn the paprika. Fry on each side for 2 minutes. Serve with the roasted capsicum emulsion, and season with sea salt flakes.

I recommend eating this with crusty bread, and some boiled kifler potato that have been sliced and brushed with remaining paprika oil.

https://youtu.be/phRVISZDJgI

Fish pie

Serves 4

The term "comfort food" is overused in food writing, but it perfectly encapsulates this dish. This is a no-frills, hearty meal, free from the pretensions of fancy ingredients, intricate garnishes, or tweezer-ing of microgreens. It's about wholesome ingredients coming together in a large casserole dish, topped generously with mashed potato, and served with love on a cold night.

For this recipe, I've chosen blue grenadier fillet, an ideal choice due to its firm texture that holds up well during cooking and its minimal bone content. Also known as cod or hoki, this fish is commonly found in the southern waters of Australia and is readily available. From a sustainability standpoint, the blue grenadier has mixed ratings. The Marine Stewardship Council and the Australian federal government deem it sustainable, but the Australian Marine Conservation Society (AMCS) rates it as yellow, suggesting it be consumed less frequently due to seal deaths associated with its fishing. You can find more information at https://goodfishbadfish.com.au/fish/blue-grenadier/. Feel free to substitute with any firm fish of your choice.

I sometimes add prawn cutlets to the dish for a burst of colour, but they are optional.

- 1 kg potatoes, peeled and cubed
- 2 large eggs
- 50 g baby spinach
- Olive oil
- 1 leek, thinly sliced
- 1 carrot, peeled and diced
- 250 ml cream
- 1 lemon, juiced
- 1 heaped tbl Dijon mustard
- 2 tbl chopped flat leaf parsley
- 8 green prawn cutlets (optional)
- 450 g of firm fish, e.g. blue grenadier, skin removed and bones removed
- Additional olive oil
- Salt and pepper to taste
- Freshly ground nutmeg

Preheat oven to 210°C fan/230°C.

Bring a large pot of salted water to the boil. Add in the potatoes and cook for 2 minutes. Gently add the eggs and continue to boil for 8 minutes.

Remove the eggs and place in a bowl of cold water.

Drain the potatoes.

Peel and quarter the eggs.

In a large frypan, heat olive oil. Gently fry leek and carrot until soft.

Whilst that is cooking, chop the fish into bite-sized pieces, checking for any small bones.

Add cream to carrot mixture and gently stir until just boiling. Remove pan from the heat and add lemon juice, mustard and parsley. Mix to combine.

Place the fish, prawns, eggs and spinach into a large casserole dish. Pour over the creamy sauce and gently mix.

Mash the potatoes. Add a little olive oil and season with salt and pepper. Add nutmeg and stir. Spread potato over the fish. Bake for 25 to 30 minutes until the potato is golden brown on top.

Serve with some fresh peas topped with butter.

https://youtu.be/pRKMi4Z59HI

Kartoffelsalat (potato salad)

Serves 8

Cooking is all about people - people you share food with, and the people you meet in life's journey.

Katrin Ogilvy was such a powerful influence in my life in the 1980s and 90s. She was the first feminist I knew, and her encouragement of me has had a profound influence on my life. It is okay to be different and more than okay to be a powerful woman.

Katrin was born in Frankfurt am Main, in Germany, and despite having lived more than half her life in Australia, she still speaks with a heavy German accent and has very European ways. She always served Kartoffelsalat on Christmas Eve, and she taught me how to make this salad. Kartoffelsalat is a traditional dish that has become my "I'll bring a salad" recipe for large gatherings. There are no rules, so you can add any flavourings you like. I prefer to add speck or boiled eggs.

- 1 kg kipfler potatoes

Dressing:
- 1 red onion, finely diced
- 3 tbl good quality vinegar (white, cider, or white wine are all good)
- 4 tbl olive oil
- 2 tbl dried mixed herbs

Optional extras:
- Diced bacon
- Diced boiled egg
- Sliced anchovy fillets
- 2 tsp mustard

Boil potatoes in their skin until cooked. Drain and allow to cool.

Combine dressing ingredients in a large bowl. Add any optional extras.

Peel potatoes and finely slice. Gradually add potatoes to the bowl, ensuring that all slices are coated with the dressing.

Refrigerate until required.
This dish is even better served the next day.

https://youtu.be/4mcdyMNO7wo

Gluten free asparagus and ricotta quiche

Serves 6-8

Quiche is one of those quintessential luncheon dishes. Great for picnics, a buffet table, or a light meal with a crisp green salad. Like many of my favourite foods, quiche's origins are French. It's a savoury tart with a pastry crust filled with a custard and pieces of cheese, meat, seafood, or vegetables.

The best pastry for quiche is shortcrust. It holds its shape and crisps up beautifully. Shortcrust is also the easiest to make at home. Ten minutes in the food processor and 30 minutes resting in the fridge is nearly as quick as defrosting a frozen pre-rolled square. I was having one of those days when filming this episode — as I placed the pastry into the dish, it broke. Not ideal for video, but it let me show a handy eggwhite trick for repairing the base. This quiche doesn't have a custardy filling, as the ricotta makes it quite thick, so there was no chance of leaking. But even with a quiche Lorraine (with bacon), the eggwhite patch trick works. A key tip: use a ball of pastry to gently ease the dough into the dish — fingers can push through and cause holes.

When I think of spring, I think of wattle in flower, daffodils dancing in neighbours' gardens, and asparagus. About 10 years ago, I planted one asparagus crown. Last year I picked over 40 spears — not counting those nibbled by garden beasties. Along with tomatoes and rhubarb, asparagus is in my top three vegetables to grow. Store-bought just doesn't have the same flavour or crispness as just-picked.

In 2014 I stayed in the Dordogne region of France, in a gîte on an asparagus farm. Monsieur was growing white asparagus, kept under black plastic until picking. He was patient with my poor French and endless questions about timing, fertiliser, and cooking. Blanched and served with parsley butter was his suggestion — and it was sublime! White spears are thicker than green or purple. Grown in darkness, they don't need peeling. Green or purple ones larger than your thumb do, as their skins can be tough.

Ricotta changes this quiche's texture and cuts the richness. It's creamy without cream — a little salty and delicious. Sometimes I sweat down a leek and some bacon strips in butter and add that too. If I do, I reduce the ricotta to 300 g.

Crust:
- 250 g plain flour (GF)
- ½ tsp xanthan gum
- 100 g butter, very cold and cut into cubes
- 1 egg yolk
- 60 ml ice water
- 20 g parmesan, grated
- 15 ml olive oil
- pinch of salt

Filling:
- 8 stalks of young asparagus
- 400 g ricotta
- 3 large eggs
- 100 g parmesan, grated
- freshly ground nutmeg
- salt and pepper

In a food processor, combine all of the flour, xanthan gum, parmesan, salt, and butter. Pulse until it resembles breadcrumbs. Add oil, egg yolk, and half of the water and work to form a smooth dough, adding water in very small amounts as needed. Wrap in clingfilm and rest in the fridge for 30 minutes.

Preheat the oven to 170°C fan/190°C.
Remove the woody ends from the asparagus.

In a medium-sized bowl, mix together the ricotta, eggs, parmesan, nutmeg, and season with salt and pepper.

Roll out the pastry to approximately 3 mm, to fit your quiche dish. Use a ball or extra pastry to gently ease the pastry into the dish, being careful not to tear the base. Chill for 10 minutes.

Arrange the asparagus in the dish in a decorative design. Gently pour in the egg mixture, spreading it evenly.

Bake for 35-40 minutes or until the top is golden and the centre is a little "jiggly". Allow it to rest for at least 15 minutes before serving. It can be served warm or at room temperature with a crisp green salad.

https://youtu.be/KOg5JuxfU0Q

New World Flavours

In the 16th century, as Europeans began exploring the globe, the phrase "New World" was used to describe the lands they discovered — primarily North and South America. Today, with North American culture so dominant, it feels a bit odd to still call it "The New World." Even what we in Australia think of as Mexican food is really Tex-Mex.

My own travels in the Americas have been limited — Argentina, a weekend in Brazil, and a few short trips to the USA. So, the recipes in this chapter aren't inspired by firsthand experiences as much as by impressions gathered from movies, books, and social media. This isn't an extensive guide to the rich and diverse cuisines of the South American continent, but rather a reflection of how these flavours have influenced my cooking.

Without the discovery of the Americas, we wouldn't have potatoes, tomatoes, maize, chocolate, or coffee — and my culinary world would look very different. The influence of this "New World" is woven into nearly every savoury dish I make. And honestly, a world without chocolate or coffee? I'd rather not think about it!

Claypots Evening Star bringing the fire to South Melbourne Market.

Gluten free apple pie with flakey pastry

Serves 6-8

Pastry is one of those things that has taken me a long time to perfect. It is one of the most disappointing things about eating gluten-free - most of the commercially produced pastries are like rubber. I have tried over the years, so many recipes using mashed potato, cooking the pastry like a roux, weird and wonderful flours etc. None worked to my satisfaction or had the family asking for seconds. Until now!

A few months ago, I was lucky enough to be involved in the Country Women's Association of Victoria baking masterclass, and although the instructor was using regular flour for the class, in the discussions afterwards, we spoke of what was really needed to get the air and flakiness in the pastry, but that could be modified to work within Gluten-Free flour's properties. So I had a play...

This is what I have come up with, and paired with Stephanie Alexander's Classic Apple Pie filling, it is a real winner!

The pastry is a little bit fiddly, and it will take you 30-45 minutes to prepare - but trust me, it's worth it!

Flaky Pastry:
- 300 g plain flour (GF)
- 1 tsp xanthan gum (optional)
- ¼ tsp salt
- 150 g cold butter, cubed
- 125 g water
- 115 g frozen butter
- Additional 115 g frozen butter
- Additional plain flour for dusting

Filling:
- 800 g apples, peeled, cored, and sliced finely
- ¼ cup brown sugar
- 2 tbl cornflour
- 1 tsp cinnamon
- Zest of 1 lemon

Egg wash:
- 1 egg, beaten

Preheat oven to 200°C fan/220°C.

Flaky Pastry:

Put flour, xanthan gum, salt, cubed butter, and water in a mixing bowl. Mix on low speed until it forms a ball.

Dust a firm surface with some extra flour. Turn out dough and knead gently until flexible.

Roll into a rectangle (about 40 x 30 cm).

Grate one frozen butter chunk over the dough (like pizza topping).

Fold one long edge over the butter, then the other. Fold one short end, then roll it all up.

Re-roll into another 40 x 30 cm rectangle, dusting underneath as needed to prevent sticking.

Fold each long edge to meet in the middle (now 40 x 15 cm). Do the same with the short edges.

Fold one side over the other like a book (10 x 15 cm). Chill for 15 minutes.

Repeat the rolling and folding once more to build up more flaky layers.

Pastry is ready to use.

Filling:

In a large bowl, mix brown sugar, cornflour, zest, and cinnamon. Add apple and toss to coat.

To assemble:

Roll out half the pastry to fit the pie dish and sides.

Gently place into the dish and ease it into place.

Spoon in the filling, mounding it slightly in the centre.

Roll out the rest of the pastry for a lid. Cover the pie and crimp edges.

Cut two slashes on top to let steam escape.

Brush with egg wash.

Bake for 20 minutes, then reduce heat to 180°C fan / 200°C and bake another 30 minutes.

Rest for at least 10 minutes before slicing.

https://youtu.be/nqz770pDCDs

Gluten free banana bread

Makes 1 loaf

It can be difficult at times to "eat out" for breakfast when you require a gluten-free diet. Recently, while travelling for work, the only gluten-free option I could find for breakfast was banana bread. It was lightly toasted and served with yoghurt. It was my 3rd cafe, and I was running out of options since I needed to reach the conference centre where I was due to present an all-day workshop. I needed something more substantial than the muesli bar I had in my bag, so I reluctantly ordered the banana bread. I must confess - I actually don't like bananas - the texture or the smell, and had, as a result, never tried banana bread before, but desperate times call for desperate measures.

Much to my great surprise, it was actually delicious! I even felt the need to double-check with the waitress that it was indeed gluten-free, given how light, fluffy, and tasty it was.

Upon my return home, I shared this experience with my gorgeous Myles, and he was very surprised. That's when my quest began for the perfect gluten-free banana bread recipe. After numerous unsuccessful attempts, I found one that required only a few minor tweaks to make the grade.

This bread has several noteworthy features:

* It freezes well - don't forget to slice it before putting it into the freezer.
* It toasts beautifully.
* It's a great way to use up bananas whose skins have turned brown from storage in the fridge.
* It travels well in a lunch box.

For best results, use a solid bread tin. This will ensure even cooking of the loaf and yield a nice crust.

- 2 cups plain flour (GF)
- 1 tsp xanthan gum
- ¾ tsp salt
- 1 tsp baking powder
- ½ tsp baking soda
- ⅔ cup white sugar
- 8 tbl coconut oil, melted and cooled
- 2 eggs, beaten
- 1 tsp vanilla extract
- 150 g Greek yoghurt
- 1 cup ripe bananas, mashed (usually 2 bananas)

Topping:
- 2 tbl coconut oil, melted
- ⅓ cup white sugar
- 2 tsp ground cinnamon

Preheat oven to 180°C fan/200°C.

Grease a bread tin.

Combine flour, xanthan gum, baking soda, baking powder, salt and sugar in a large bowl. Mix well. Add the coconut oil, eggs, vanilla and then yoghurt, mixing well between each ingredient. Gently add the mashed bananas.

Combine all the topping ingredients together in a small bowl.

Place half the batter into your bread tin. Ensure that layer is even. Spread a thin layer of the topping (about half of the mixture). Top with remaining batter and even out. Top with remaining topping and spread evenly.

Bake in the centre of the oven for 45 minutes. Lower the oven to 160°C and bake for another 10 minutes.

Allow the banana bread to cool in the tin.

Blueberry buttermilk pancakes

Makes 12

I love pancakes on a Sunday morning for brunch. It is one of the sad things about being coeliac, that despite gluten-free buttermilk pancakes being so easy to make, very few cafes sell them. I often watch longingly as Myles enjoys them - although he never puts enough maple syrup on them for my liking.

This recipe is easy to make up the night before and in the morning add the beaten egg whites and cook. To be honest, I'm never that organised :)

The secret ingredient to getting those light fluffy pancakes is buttermilk. Traditionally, buttermilk was referred to as the liquid left over from churning cream into butter. Buttermilk is thicker than normal milk as the lactose contained in the milk ferments. This also gives it a slightly acidic taste and decreases the pH. The lactic acid then reacts with the bicarb soda to produce carbon dioxide - making the pancakes light and fluffy, even when using gluten-free flours. Trust me - the family won't be able to pick that these are gluten-free!

NB: If you don't have access to buttermilk, just add the juice of half a lemon to the regular milk. It starts the fermenting process and will give you a similar effect to that of the buttermilk.

- 3 eggs
- 2 cups buttermilk
- 60 g butter, melted
- 300 g plain flour (GF)
- 1 tsp salt
- 1 tsp bicarbonate of soda
- 1 punnet of blueberries
- Additional butter for frying

Separate the eggs. In a medium-sized bowl, beat egg yolks well. Whisk in buttermilk and melted butter. Sift in flour, salt and bicarbonate of soda. Gently fold in the dry ingredients.

In a separate bowl, whisk egg whites until soft peaks are achieved. Fold into the prepared batter (It will be lumpy - don't overbeat).

Lightly grease a heavy-based frypan. Ladle in ¼ cup of batter. Cook until bubbles appear on the top (a little like a crumpet). Sprinkle with a few blueberries, then gently flip. Cook on the second side for 2-3 minutes. Keep cooked pancakes warm until all are cooked.

Serve with real maple syrup and natural yoghurt.

https://youtu.be/6FKQ3m1A4d4

Chocolate brownies

Makes 12

I was lucky enough to receive a laser thermometer for Christmas and decided to do some baking experiments with it. The recipe I chose to experiment with is Chocolate Brownies, a treat for afternoon tea and handy for school lunchboxes as well.

The experiments used both a silicone baking tray and a metal baking tray. Three batches of gluten-free chocolate brownies were made, and the differences in the results were quite remarkable. It just goes to show that you need to be familiar with your oven and equipment. Trial and error does work.

Trial 1: Using a silicone tray and ⅔ of the recipe, the tray was cooled for 30 minutes before turning out of the tin. It stuck!

Trial 2: Using a metal tray lined with baking paper and the full recipe. The tray was cooled for 30 minutes before turning out of the tin. It did not stick but broke up when lifted out.

Trial 3: Using a metal tray lined with baking paper and the full recipe. The tray was cooled for 1.5 hours before turning out of the tin. When it originally came out of the oven, the brownie was 114°C. After 30 minutes, it had dropped to 40°C. At an hour out of the oven, it was 30°C, and after the 1.5-hour mark, it had cooled to room temperature (24°C). Lifting it out now and cutting it into squares was successful.

This was a valuable lesson in gluten-free baking. I always "knew" that I needed to let baked goods cool in the tray but had sometimes cheated and rushed to get them out and onto a cooling rack. This has often led to items crumbling, and I was never sure why. So now I know!

- 105 g butter
- 150 g dark chocolate
- 255 g caster sugar
- 3 eggs, lightly beaten
- 105 g rice flour
- 1½ tsp baking powder
- ¼ tsp salt
- ¾ tsp vanilla extract
- 105 g macadamia nuts, chopped

Preheat oven to 160°C fan/180°C.

Line a 28 cm square tin with baking paper.

Melt the butter and chocolate together in a double boiler over a low heat, stirring constantly. Remove from the heat and add the sugar. Mix well. Allow to cool.

Add the eggs. Mix well.

Sift in the flour, baking powder and salt. Mix well.

Fold in the vanilla and nuts.

Pour the mixture into the baking tin and bake for 35 minutes.

Allow to cool completely in the tin.

Cut into squares to serve.

https://youtu.be/TsnILLi9kig

Chocolate lava cake

Makes 4

2023 was the year generative AI and ChatGPT hit the spotlight — an odd way to start a food blog, I know! Over the summer break, my partner Myles began experimenting with ChatGPT. I was sceptical, especially when he showed me the AI's 2023 recipe list. Despite tweaking prompts based on our 90 past recipes, ChatGPT insisted we add chocolate lava cake—highlighting an amusing bias in its early model.

Truth be told, I'd never made a chocolate lava cake and could only picture Jon Favreau's character in Chef, fuming when customers demanded his signature dish. To keep the peace at home, I decided to try it.

There are two main methods for lava cake. The more common one involves barely baking the outside in a hot oven (sometimes in a bain-marie) to create that molten centre. My results were often mousse-like—not quite the ooze I'd hoped for. I doubt that gluten-free flour was the issue.

The second method, which I prefer, uses a ganache ball in the centre. This guarantees a rich molten core—even when reheated the next day.

Some recipes recommend very dark chocolate, but I found 70% cocoa makes the cake stodgy, without improving the flavour. Dark choc chips with 50% cocoa work well and are easy to find.

Getting the cakes out of the moulds was tricky. They tasted great but weren't as visually striking (though if it breaks, maybe the calories fall out?). To avoid this, grease the moulds with melted butter, dust with cocoa, and chill before filling. After baking, let them rest 5 minutes before serving—especially with gluten-free flour. Since the recipe uses just a little flour, you can easily swap in your go-to GF blend without xanthan gum.

These chocolate lava cakes are an easy, show-stopping dessert. I hope you enjoy making them as much as I did.

Chocolate ganache:
- 110 g dark chocolate chips (50% cocoa)
- 80 ml heavy/thickened cream

Mold preparation:
- 5 g butter, melted
- 1 tbl cocoa

Cake batter:
- 200 g dark chocolate chips (50% cocoa)
- 100 g unsalted butter, cubed
- 2 eggs, at room temperature
- 2 egg yolks, at room temperature
- 65 g caster sugar
- 2 tbl plain flour (GF)

To serve:
- Ice cream or cream (highly recommended!)
- Cocoa for dusting

Ganache:

Place chocolate and cream in a microwave-safe bowl. Microwave on high for three 20-second bursts, stirring in between, until smooth.

Cool for 10 minutes, then refrigerate for 3 hours or until firm enough to scoop.

Cake:

Preheat oven to 190°C fan/210°C.

Grease 4 x 170ml dariole or pudding moulds with melted butter, dust with cocoa, tap out excess, and chill on a tray.

Place chocolate and butter in a microwave-safe bowl. Microwave in 30-second bursts, stirring in between. Stir until smooth, then cool for 5 minutes.

In a separate bowl, whisk eggs, yolks, and sugar until frothy and sugar has dissolved.

Add cooled chocolate mixture and mix until combined.

Fold in flour until just incorporated—don't over-mix.

Fill moulds one-third full.

Add a heaped teaspoon of ganache to the centre, then top with more batter, leaving 1cm from the top. Repeat.

Bake for 20 minutes, or until the tops spring back when gently touched.

Let sit for 5 minutes, then turn out. Tap the base with a spoon and gently remove the mould.

Serve with ice cream or cream, a dusting of cocoa.

https://youtu.be/x1Xee0YvN8s

Gluten free pancakes & strawberries

Makes 8-10

Every culture has a form of pancake in their traditional cuisine. To name just a few: North America has flapjacks, Australia has pikelets, Japan has Okonomiyaki, Austria has Kaiserschmarrn, France has Crêpes, Brazil has Tapiocas, Colombia has Arepas, Denmark has Æbleskiver, Ethiopia has Injera, Greece has Tiganites and Britain has pancakes. Some are always sweet, some always savoury and some are versatile to be served either way.

English pancakes are much thinner than their North American counterpart. They are slightly thicker than French crêpes and are traditionally topped with sugar and a squeeze of lemon. These pancakes are often eaten on Shrove Tuesday, in preparation for Lent to mark Easter, though they are also enjoyed throughout the year.

- 150 g gluten-free self-raising flour
- 80 g white rice flour
- 85 g caster sugar
- 40 g buckwheat flour
- 300 ml milk
- 2 eggs, lightly beaten
- 60 g butter, melted
- Additional butter for cooking
- Shredded coconut, lightly toasted
- Chia seeds
- 1 punnet of strawberries

Sift together flours. Stir in the sugar. Whisk together milk, eggs and butter. Make a well in the centre of the flours and add the milk mixture. Whisk until smooth. Allow batter to rest for 5-10 minutes.

Lightly grease a non-stick pan with butter. Pour in approximately ¼ cup of the batter. Gently fry until bubbles appear on the top. Flip pancake and cook for 2-3 minutes until brown. Remove from pan and keep warm whilst cooking the remaining pancakes.

Wash and hull strawberries, slice in half. Place in small pan with 1 tbl water. Gently cook until syrupy.

To serve, place 2-3 pancakes on a large plate. Spoon over strawberries and sprinkle with chia seeds and toasted coconut.

https://youtu.be/OUw2qlvFwWQ

Gluten free red velvet cupcakes

Makes 12

Confession time: I've always made cupcakes using packet mix. Even after being diagnosed with coeliac disease, I stuck with supermarket gluten-free brands—but they were often dry and dense.

My good friend Carol was a brilliant baker. She once entered a cupcake bake-off at the Country Women's Association of Victoria's fair and wowed MasterChef judge Matt Preston so much he published her recipe (with permission!). Carol's method broke the rules—no creaming butter and sugar—and we often talked about adapting bakes to be gluten-free. Using her recipe as a base, I've made tweaks to create a moist, light cupcake. Sadly, Carol never saw this version—but I think she'd approve.

There are a few ways to make red velvet cake: with beetroot juice for natural colouring, with buttermilk and vinegar reacting with natural cocoa, or with red food colouring. I prefer the food colouring method — it's the most consistent.

My friend Penny gave me a great tip: use an ice cream scoop for even cupcakes. Mine holds 45 ml (3 tbl, #12), but scoop sizes vary from 8 ml to 250 ml.

Patty cases come in mini, standard, or jumbo sizes. I use standard ones to fit my tin and prefer thicker paper to help prevent butter stains. If staining does occur, I simply place the cooled cupcake—wrapper and all—into a fresh, clean case for a neater finish.

I use plain gluten-free flour with added raising agents — it gives me better results than self-raising gluten-free flour with xanthan gum, which I found too inconsistent, especially across different flour blends.

Let cakes cool in the tin for 5 minutes, then on a wire rack. Store only once fully cool to prevent sweating, which can loosen wrappers.

Ice only once cool. Red velvet is often topped with cream cheese or Ermine buttercream, but I prefer chocolate buttercream. Bring to room temp before piping. Decorated cupcakes keep well for 3 days at room temp.

- 200 g plain flour (GF)
- 20 g cocoa powder
- 230 g caster sugar
- 2 tsp baking powder
- 1 tsp bicarbonate of soda
- 1 tsp xanthan gum
- 1 tsp vanilla extract
- ¼ tsp sea salt
- 125 g butter, at room temperature and cubed
- 2 eggs (110 g out of shell), at room temp
- 150 ml milk
- 3 tsp red food colouring

Buttercream Icing:
- 80 g butter softened
- 260 g icing sugar
- 60 g cocoa
- ⅓ cup milk
- 2 tsp vanilla extract
- ¼ tsp sea salt

Preheat oven to 150°C fan-forced.

Line a 12 patty tin with paper cases.

Sift together flour, cocoa, baking powder, bicarbonate, salt and xanthan gum into a large bowl. Add in butter, sugar and using an electric mixer, beat on low speed for 1 minute. Add eggs, vanilla and combine well. Combine milk and red food colouring in a jug. Slowly add milk to the bowl, and then on low continue to mix for 5 minutes until pale.

Using an ice-cream scoop (45 ml) to make them even place the mixture into the patty cases (Should fill them about ⅔).

Bake for 35 minutes until a skewer comes out clean.

Allow to sit in the tin for 5 minutes before transferring to a wire rack to cool.

Chocolate Buttercream Icing

In the bowl of a stand mixer fitted with the paddle attachment, beat the butter on medium speed until it is smooth, for about 1 minute.

Add the icing sugar and cocoa powder to the bowl and beat until combined. With the stand mixer running on low speed, slowly stream in the milk and vanilla extract then add the salt and continue beating until well combined, scraping down the sides as needed, for about 2 minutes.

Increase the speed to high and beat the icing for an additional 2 minutes. Place into a piping bag fitted with a large star nozzle and decorate your cooled cupcakes.

Gluten free waffles

Makes 6

Who can resist a crispy, yet light and fluffy waffle with summer berries, mascarpone, and maple syrup? Certainly not me! They are definitely a special treat. My sister-in-law serves them up on Christmas morning for breakfast. I certainly enjoy them all year round. It has taken a little bit of trial and error to get the gluten-free batter "just right" in order to share it with you all.

Waffles are best eaten still warm from the waffle iron. The gluten-free batter doesn't keep well, but if you have any cooked waffles left over, they can be frozen for another day. To reheat, place in your toaster on the "frozen" setting.

Each waffle iron has its own properties. I use a Tefal, with interchangeable plates. It cooks two (2) at a time, which is perfect for Myles and me. I use half a cup of mixture per waffle. It is important not to overfill the plate, as the batter can just ooze out the sides and make quite a mess.

It is OK to use a commercial gluten-free plain flour, but as they vary so much between brands, I have broken down the flour into the specific flours, as I want to make sure you get a consistent, crisp outside and fluffy inside each time.

The addition of natural yoghurt to the batter gives a lighter batter too. If you are wanting a dairy-free option, skip the yoghurt and add an extra 30 mls of dairy-free milk.

- 95 g rice flour
- 30 g potato flour
- 15 g tapioca flour
- ¾ tsp baking powder (GF)
- ¼ tsp baking soda
- ¼ tsp salt
- 1 egg, separated
- 1½ tbl vegetable oil
- ½ cup yoghurt
- 90 ml milk

Combine all flours, baking powder, baking soda, and salt in a large bowl.

In a separate bowl whisk the egg white until firm peaks.

In a third bowl, beat the egg yolk and oil until well combined. Add yoghurt and milk and blend together.

Add the yoghurt mix to the dry ingredients and mix well. Gently fold in the egg whites.

Preheat your waffle iron. Add ½ cup of batter to each iron. There is no need to spread the batter out, as the top iron will do this for you. Cook for 4 minutes*.

Serve with your choice of mixed berries, banana, Nutella, mascarpone, yoghurt, maple syrup.

* Cooking time will vary between waffle irons. Waffles are cooked when the steam stops escaping.

https://youtu.be/tcTGpKAMMFs

Chicken enchiladas

Makes 6-8

My Chicken Enchilada recipe isn't authentic Mexican. It probably aligns more closely with Tex-Mex. But regardless of the nationality, they're unquestionably delicious!

Traditionally, enchiladas are made with a corn tortilla, as opposed to a burrito which is typically made with a flour tortilla. This makes enchiladas a gluten-free alternative. An enchilada is defined as a corn tortilla stuffed with meat and covered with a tomato and chilli sauce (The Real Academia Española). Fortunately, corn tortillas are becoming more readily available in shops, but if you prefer to make your own, as I sometimes do, here is a link to my tortilla recipe and quesadillas. The sauce is easily made with ingredients found in the pantry and is tastier than the packet mixes you can buy, with no added preservatives.

As for the cheese, it doesn't really matter what type you use. I prefer a 50:50 mix of mature tasty and smoked cheddar.

When it comes to preparing the chicken, I prefer to use two forks to pull apart the seared fillets. There's nothing wrong with cutting the fillets into small pieces either. I prefer thigh fillets in this recipe - they're juicier and more flavourful. But I understand many people only eat the white meat, and so one chicken large breast will be just as suitable too.

This recipe allows for a lot of customisation to suit your family's preferences. You could easily add some black beans, or substitute the chicken with beef or pork. A quick guacamole, made from mashed avocado, lime juice and ¼ tsp of chilli powder, could replace the salsa if you prefer.

- 5 tbl lime juice
- 2 cloves garlic, crushed
- 2 tsp garlic powder
- 2 tsp onion powder
- 2 tsp dried oregano
- 3 tsp cumin powder
- 3 tsp smoked paprika
- ½ tsp cayenne pepper
- 1 tsp salt
- 4 chicken thighs
- Olive oil
- 2 tbl tomato paste
- 2 tsp sugar
- 1 cup chicken stock
- 8 corn tortillas
- 500 g grated cheese

- Sour cream
- 1 batch of fresh salsa

Preheat oven to 160°C fan/180°C.

Combine 3 tablespoon lime juice, garlic, garlic powder, onion powder, oregano, cumin, paprika, cayenne pepper, salt and 2 tablespoon chicken stock in a large bowl. Stir well. Add chicken and toss to coat well.

In a heavy-based frypan, heat a little olive oil. Add chicken and cook for 3-4 minutes on each side. Remove chicken and add to the frypan the tomato paste, sugar, chicken stock and any of the marinade dregs from the large bowl. Stir to combine and bring to a slow simmer.

Shred the chicken (don't worry if it is not fully cooked inside at this point).

Return chicken to the frypan and stir to coat with the sauce. Cook for 3-5 minutes.

Warm tortillas in the microwave as per packet directions (Usually 30-60 seconds).

On a board, place 1 tablespoon of chicken into the centre of each tortilla. Sprinkle a handful of cheese over chicken. Fold the tortilla over, and place fold down into a large baking dish. Repeat until all are made.

Add 1-2 tablespoon of lime juice to the remaining sauce. Cover all tortillas with sauce. Top with remaining cheese. Bake for 15-20 minutes until cheese is melted and brown.

Serve with sour cream and fresh salsa.

My fresh Salsa:
- 1 corn cob
- 1 avocado diced
- 150 g tomatoes diced
- ½ bunch coriander chopped fine
- 1 tbl fresh lime juice
- 1 fresh jalapeno chilli chopped finely

Microwave corn for 1 minute until just tender. Using a sharp knife, remove kernels from the cob. Allow to cool.

Combine all ingredients in a small bowl and serve.

Gluten free quesadilla

Serves 8

"Cornflour just ain't cornflour" - many are surprised that cornflour isn't always made from corn, so when baking gluten-free, you always need to check the ingredients.

Gluten is found in wheat, oats, barley, and rye. Corn (or maize) is gluten-free. So where does the mix-up come from? Well, in the UK, "cornflour" is a generic term referring to flour made from grain. Therefore, some cornflours are made from wheat! In Australia, the common brands are Keens and Nurses. Both of which are made from wheat and ARE NOT GLUTEN-FREE! Luckily, there are plenty of other brands whose cornflour is made from corn and therefore is gluten-free.

Cornflour also comes in many grades. Most cooks are familiar with the white starchy flour commonly used to thicken sauces (and called corn starch in the USA), the yellow maize flour, and polenta. All of these are available in the usual grocery stores. The star ingredient used in this episode is Masa flour. This flour is commonly used in Mexican, Central, and South American cooking. It is sometimes referred to as masa harina. The flour comes in white, yellow, and blue depending on the type of corn used and the level of refinement it goes through. Masa flour is significantly different from all the other forms of cornflour because, due to the addition of lime in the refining process, the resulting flour has the ability to form a dough (not just a paste). Masa flour can then form tortillas! Masa flour can be purchased from specialty shops.

Quesadillas are a wonderful snack or light lunch. They can be made with any filling, and I highly recommend making them with my homemade salsa (Once you have tried it fresh, you will never buy it in a jar again!). Enjoy!

Tortilla:
- 2 cups masa flour
- 225-250 ml water
- ¼ tsp salt
- Vegetable oil (or butter)

Filling:
- 1 small tin black beans
- 1 small tin corn kernels
- 1 cup salsa
- 1.5 cups grated cheese (cheddar or tasty)

Salsa:
- 1 large tin tomatoes
- 1 small tin tomatoes
- ½ onion, chopped finely
- 1 fresh jalapeño, sliced finely
- 1 bunch coriander
- ¼ tsp each of salt, black pepper, cumin, and sugar
- Juice of 1 lime

Salsa:
Using a food processor, blend all salsa ingredients to the desired consistency. Chill until ready to assemble quesadillas.

Filling:
Combine all ingredients in a small bowl.

Tortilla:
Combine flour, water and salt in a bowl - use a dinner knife to stir.

Mix to a firm dough. Cover with cling film and allow to rest for 5-10 minutes.

Divide the dough into 16. Roll each section into a ball.

Flatten between layers of baking paper (cartouche) in a tortilla press.

In a hot non-stick pan, fry each tortilla for 2-3 minutes on each side. Keep warm until all tortillas are made.

Place one tortilla in a hot pan brushed with oil. Spread salsa over the tortilla. Place one tablespoon of fillings on the tortilla.

Cover with the second tortilla and fry on each side until golden brown and cheese is melted.

Serve with extra salsa, guacamole and sour cream.

https://youtu.be/H5SVeKMYa3w

Spice and Silk

For at least the first half of my life, despite Australia's location in the Asia-Pacific, our national identity felt far more European — with a touch of cowboy — than Asian. The sun-tanned Aussie, laid-back, sports-loving, with a irreverent sense of humour and a quiet achiever mentality. The iconic images of surf lifesavers at Bondi, outback horsemen, and helicopters mustering cattle across vast open land don't truly reflect the reality of modern Australia.

Our Indigenous population is believed to have migrated from Asia around 70,000 years ago, forming the longest continuous living culture in the world. Travel between Australia and the nations of the Pacific has continued for centuries. When gold was discovered in Victoria in the 1850s, the first large wave of Chinese immigration began. Melbourne's Chinatown was established by 1851, primarily as a provisions hub for men heading to the goldfields. However, the first Chinese-born landowner in Australia was a free settler who purchased land near Parramatta in 1818.

With each wave of immigration, Australia's food landscape has evolved. According to the 2021 census, 17% of Australians have Asian heritage, with the largest groups coming from China and India. Their influence on Australian cuisine has been profound — there isn't a food court in the country without at least one Asian outlet, often serving sushi or Indian curries. Chinese, Thai, Vietnamese, Japanese, Indian, Malaysian, and Korean cuisines have become staples in Australian dining. As cultural integration deepens, Australians are becoming more knowledgeable about the regional distinctions within these cuisines. While we still tend to "Anglicise" dishes — dialling down spice levels or omitting ingredients like chicken feet — the availability of authentic ingredients has improved dramatically. Many Asian pantry staples can now be found in mainstream supermarkets, with specialty stores catering to the more niche ingredients.

My own travels in Asia have mainly centred on Japan, but I've been fortunate to have friends and family with Asian heritage who have shared their knowledge, tips, and treasured recipes with me.

A bustling laneway in Dotonbori at night, Osaka, Japan

Black pepper chicken

Serves 3-4

One of the most challenging aspects of being diagnosed with Coeliac disease as an adult is coming to terms with all the foods you once relished but can no longer have. Among these is the simple pleasure of dropping by the local Chinese takeaway for a hot meal ready in minutes. We all have our favourites — my grandmother Nancy always chose chicken and cashews, my dad loved beef with black bean sauce, Myles is partial to a combination omelette, and I'm fond of pepper chicken with steamed rice.

The techniques used in Chinese cooking are relatively easy to master: keep the food moving and the heat high. Avoid overcrowding the pan to prevent stewing instead of stir-frying. A wok makes things easier, but a large frying pan will do. A rice cooker adds "set and forget" convenience and steams rice to perfection every time.

Some ingredients can be a little elusive—often not available at local supermarkets but usually found in Asian grocers, which are a treasure trove of exciting sights, aromas and tastes. Today's recipe calls for Sichuan peppercorns and Shaoxing wine. Shaoxing is a Chinese rice wine, traditionally made with wheat. It's amber in colour with a mildly sweet aroma. If a gluten-free version isn't available, dry sherry makes a good substitute. Sichuan pepper comes from the husks of two citrus-family shrubs. These pinkish husks bring a fragrant, numbing, tongue-tingling sensation and earthy flavour. It's also the key ingredient in Chinese five spice.

In traditional pepper chicken, the Sichuan to black pepper ratio is 1:1. I've used 1:2, as Myles isn't fond of the tingling from hydroxy-alpha-sanshool, the compound that activates nerve receptors in your mouth. Adjust the ratio to suit your family's preferences. Even a small amount of Sichuan pepper enhances the dish.

This recipe makes more seasoning than needed. Store the rest in an airtight container for up to three months—it's fantastic on grilled chicken or seafood. I prefer using my granite mortar and pestle, which leaves a bit of texture. A spice grinder works too, but gives a finer finish.

- 3 boneless, skinless chicken thigh fillets
- ½ cup corn flour (GF)
- 1 brown onion, diced
- 1 red capsicum, diced
- Vegetable oil for shallow frying, plus 1 tbl extra

Black pepper sauce:
- ½ tbl whole Sichuan peppercorns
- 1 tbl whole black peppercorns
- ¼ cup oyster sauce (GF)
- 2 tbl Chinese Shaoxing wine
- 1 tsp dark soy sauce (GF)

Marinade:
- 1 tbl soy sauce (GF)
- 1 garlic clove, finely grated

Cut the chicken into bite-sized pieces.

Into a medium-sized bowl combine all the marinade ingredients and stir well. Add the chicken and stir to coat. Cover the bowl and put aside for later.

Place the Sichuan peppercorns in a small frypan over high heat. Cook, shaking the pan, for 2 minutes or until the peppercorns are fragrant and just starting to smoke. Transfer to a mortar along with the black peppercorns. Grind to a fine powder.

In a small bowl, mix 1 tablespoon of the peppercorn powder with the oyster sauce, Shaoxing wine and dark soy sauce.

Add about a centimetre of oil to the base of a wok over a high heat. When the oil is hot (170°C), toss a quarter of the marinated chicken in the cornflour until lightly coated. Shake off excess flour and then cook in the oil for 3-4 minutes or until golden and cooked through. Drain on paper towel. Repeat with the remaining chicken and flour.

Heat the 1 tablespoon of oil in a large wok over a high heat. Add the onion and capsicum and stir-fry for a minute. Add the chicken and the peppercorn sauce and stir-fry until well combined and warmed through. Serve immediately with steamed rice and Asian greens of your choice.

Chicken basil stir fry

Serves 4

When it's been a long day at work, sometimes you just need a quick recipe that can feed an army, and warms you through. The wonderful combination of crisp vegetables, creamy coconut, with the zing of chilli and umami of fish sauce fits this bill to a tee. In 20 minutes you can be curled up on the couch, holding a steaming bowl of rice, this stir fry and the world will seem a better place.

The nature of stir fry is a quick action to seal all the goodness in the meat and maintain the nutritional value of the vegetables. There is no rule on what vegetables to use - whatever is in season or at hand. I love snow peas, baby corn, bok choy, bean sprouts, porcini mushrooms and the colour of red capsicum - so I have used them all.

I have used my well-loved wok to cook this dish. I have owned this wonderful, and frankly, indispensable, piece of cooking equipment for close to thirty years. It is made of carbon steel and has two handles - this makes it easy to handle and move food quickly. This style is common in Southern China. My wok has a flat bottom - designed to sit better on western stoves. You can also get woks made of cast iron or aluminium, electric and non-stick. Whatever your wok is made from, keep it well-seasoned (oil it after washing, before putting it away to prevent rust). You will get many years of use from this simple tool, that is not only great for stir-frys, but also for steaming, deep frying, smoking or braising.

- 4 chicken thigh fillets
- 2 garlic cloves, crushed
- 1 chili, thinly sliced
- 2 cm fresh ginger, grated
- 4 spring onions, sliced
- ½ capsicum, sliced
- 120 g porcini mushrooms, sliced
- 75 g snow peas
- 60 g baby corn
- 3 bunches bok choy, roughly chopped
- 75 g bean sprouts
- 2 tbl fish sauce
- ½ bunch Thai basil
- 300 ml coconut cream
- Oil for cooking

- Steamed rice to serve

Prepare all vegetables into bite-sized pieces.
Cut chicken into 2cm square pieces.

Cook rice as per packet instructions.

Heat wok. Add 2 tablespoons of oil. When oil starts to smoke, add half of the chicken. Toss continually to seal all the pieces. When sealed, remove chicken and repeat with remaining chicken pieces.

When the second batch is sealed, return all chicken to the wok and add chilli, ginger and garlic. Continuing to toss, add thicker vegetables - bok choy, corn, capsicum. Stir-fry for 3-4 minutes.

Add fish sauce to the wok, along with spring onion, snow peas and mushrooms. Add coconut cream and toss through. As the sauce thickens, add thai basil and bean sprouts for the final crunch. Stir to warm through.

Serve with steamed rice.

https://youtu.be/ikPzqwAf1Q8

Crispy yuan salmon

Serves 2

The Japanese certainly appreciate the subtleties of cooking fish - or not cooking fish, as the case may be. Myles and I have been fortunate enough to visit Japan on three separate occasions. In 2018, we had the opportunity to visit the Tsukiji fish market in Tokyo, the largest wholesale fish market in the world and an absolute paradise for foodies! Although we didn't rise before sunrise to witness the famous tuna auction, we spent a day wandering around the bustling outer market, sampling numerous delicacies "on a stick", sashimi, and seafood dishes from a wide variety of vendors. We only managed to cover about three quarters of the vendors before our legs gave out. We'll definitely return on our next visit to Tokyo.

Yuan marinade is a simple mixture made from readily available ingredients. It enhances the flavour of the salmon, but can also add a subtle flavour to white fish or chicken. You might not have mirin in your pantry (though I strongly recommend that you do). It lends a subtle sweetness and umami flavour to a variety of Japanese dishes including teriyaki and ramen. Mirin is a sweet rice wine with a lower alcohol content than sake (usually around 14%). I can find mirin in the Asian food aisle at my local supermarket.

The crispy skin of the salmon is not a feature of the dish that I encountered in Japan. My Western palate loves the crisp snap of the skin, so I cook it skin-side down first to ensure utmost crispness. Traditional Japanese recipes suggest cooking it skin-side up first, merely searing the skin. The choice is yours.

For serving, I recommend some crisp stir-fried greens and a steaming bowl of jasmine rice.

- 2 salmon fillets, skin on
- 5 tbl mirin
- 3 tbl soy sauce (GF)
- 2 tbl sake
- Juice of ½ lime

Pat the pieces of salmon dry with kitchen paper towel. Check to ensure all small bones have been removed.

In a shallow dish, mix together all remaining ingredients. Lay the salmon, skin side up, in a single layer in the dish. Try to avoid letting any of the marinade touch the skin. Gently wipe it away with paper towel if it does.

Heat a heavy frypan. Place the salmon skin side down. You should hear a sizzle that suggests the pan is hot enough. Cook until the fillet shows a colour change up to two-thirds of the thickness. This is usually 4-8 minutes depending on the thickness of your fish fillet.

Flip the fillet using an egg-slide to keep the fillet together in a nice piece, and cook for another 1-3 minutes. It should still be pink in the middle when you cut it. Serve the salmon skin side up to maintain the crispiness of the skin.

https://youtu.be/E4V0HYM16pE

Curried mussels (Goan style)

Serves 2

There are many myths surrounding the wonderful mollusc — the mussel.

I'm fortunate to have been invited to demonstrate mussel cooking at the Portarlington Mussel Festival each January. For 13 years, I've shown how easy mussels are to prepare. If you haven't attended, here are my top 5 tips:

1. Fresh mussels can be stored in the fridge for 7–10 days. Keep them covered with a damp tea towel, refreshed every 2–3 days.

2. Soak mussels in cool water for 20 minutes before cooking. This allows them to open and release grit and seawater.

3. De-bearding: The hard way is pulling the beard down firmly towards the rounded end. The easy way is to steam mussels in an empty pan for 3–5 minutes, then remove the beards with a gentle tug. Strain any leftover liquid and freeze — it's great for risotto or paella.

4. Many wrongly believe mussels that don't open during cooking are unsafe. This is TOTALLY INCORRECT. They're all dead — you just cooked them! The key is checking before cooking:

   a) Discard any with broken shells — you don't know how long they've been exposed.

   b) Tap any open, uncooked mussels on the bench. If they slowly close, they're good to cook. Discard those that stay open.

Mussels cook fast, and today's recipe features a quick sauce, making the dish ready in under 30 minutes — ideal for weeknights.

Goa, in South West India, is known for its beaches and tropical climate. Seafood is central to the cuisine. Goan curries, often found in Melbourne Indian restaurants, are rich and aromatic — blending spices with garlic, ginger, and coconut, and often using tomato, tamarind, or mango powder (amchur) for a sweet-sour balance.

- 1 kg fresh mussels
- 1 onion, chopped
- 2 cm piece of fresh ginger, grated or 2 tsp minced ginger
- 4 cloves garlic, crushed
- 2 green chillies, chopped
- ½ tsp ground turmeric
- 1 tsp mustard seeds (black preferred, but brown or yellow are ok)
- 2 tsp ground cumin
- 270 ml coconut milk
- Olive oil
- Salt and pepper

To serve: steamed rice, lime wedges, and fresh coriander.

Place mussels in a sink of cold water for about 20 minutes to rinse. Discard any with broken shells or that stay open when tapped.

Place the mussels in a large pan in a single layer, cover with a lid and on a medium heat cook for 4-5 minutes until the mussels have opened. Remove from the pan. Using a knife, carefully open any that had not opened. Remove the beards from all the mussels, and half the shell - leaving the mussel in the half shell to serve.

In a large frypan, heat oil. Gently fry onions until just starting to colour. Add ginger, garlic, chillies, spices, salt and pepper. Cook for 3-4 minutes until fragrant.

Add coconut milk and stir well. Bring to a simmer for 3-4 minutes.

Add the half-shell mussels to the pan and stir to warm through.

Serve on a bed of steamed rice, with the chopped coriander scattered on top and lime wedges on the side.

https://youtu.be/qZ2gHkhB1Ug

Goat curry

Serves 4-6

While goat is considered a delicacy worldwide, it hasn't been readily available in Australian butchers and supermarkets until recently. Thankfully, this is changing, and this wonderfully tender and healthier red meat, lower in cholesterol and fat than lamb or beef, is now accessible in mainstream outlets. Slowly cooking the curry over low heat ensures the meat remains tender and moist.

When making curries or stews, I always prefer to use meat on the bone. As the meat heats up, the bone marrow releases juices, adding a depth of flavour to the dish. The released collagen and albumin also contribute to the 'luscious' mouthfeel and texture of the finished dish. There's plenty of literature suggesting that 'bone-in meat' is healthier - including the added Vitamin A from the bone marrow and the release of collagen and gelatin, important for gut health. Not only that, these cuts are often cheaper and, most importantly, the resulting dish tastes better.

This curry utilises fennel - a herb that I grow in my garden with a wonderful aniseed aroma. When the seeds are dry-roasted and then ground to a fine powder, they add depth to this curry. Just a small word of caution - don't try to eat the cinnamon bark - it's quite unpalatable but contributes to the earthy tones of this curry.

I've used both chilli powder and a whole cayenne chilli in this recipe. You can, of course, modify the chilli to suit your personal preference. The chilli powder provides the heat, while the whole chilli gives the chilli flavour without the intensity.

Ideal in the colder months, this curry should be served with steamed rice and your choice of vegetables.

- 1.5 kg goat pieces (preferably on the bone)
- 1 tsp ground turmeric
- Salt and pepper, to taste
- 1 brown onion
- 10 cloves garlic
- 5 cm piece fresh ginger
- 2 tbl fennel seeds
- 2 cinnamon sticks
- 2 tbl olive oil
- 1 red chilli, chopped
- 2 tsp chilli powder
- 500 ml water
- 250 ml coconut cream
- 1 tsp caster sugar
- Juice of 1 lemon

In a large bowl, mix together the goat, turmeric and salt and pepper.

In a food processor, blend the onion, garlic and ginger into a coarse paste.

In a dry pan on a low heat, cook the fennel seeds until fragrant. Using a mortar and pestle, grind the fennel seeds to a fine powder. Break up the cinnamon sticks using the mortar and pestle.

In a large, heavy-based pot, heat the oil. Gently fry the onion and ginger paste until fragrant - 2-3 minutes. Add the fennel, chilli powder, cinnamon sticks and cook for another 2-3 minutes. Add the goat pieces and cook for 10 minutes, stirring often to coat the meat in the spice mix.

Add the whole chilli, coconut cream and water. Stir well. Bring to a simmer, and cook with the lid on, stirring occasionally for 60-90 minutes until the meat is falling off the bone.

Add the sugar and lemon juice. Stir well.
Serve with steamed rice.

https://youtu.be/QQwb3lCJnh8

Okonomiyaki

Makes 4

During a foodie tour in Japan a few years ago, we ate some phenomenal food! One of the dishes on our must-try list was Okonomiyaki prepared in the traditional Kansai style. We were fortunate enough to visit Okonomi-mura in Hiroshima. This is essentially an Okonomiyaki village, featuring multiple floors with 24 different Okonomiyaki restaurants, each with their own unique specialities. It was an amazing experience. The chef didn't speak English and I don't speak Japanese, but the universal language of food prevailed. The meals are prepared and cooked right in front of you! We enjoyed Okonomiyaki across Japan; it is often served in restaurants or by street vendors. Although typically made with wheat flour, this dish can easily be converted to gluten-free by directly swapping with gluten-free plain flour.

The name Okonomiyaki is derived from the word 'okonomi', which translates to "how you like" or "what you like", and 'yaki' meaning "cooked" (usually grilled). It typically includes cabbage, eggs and flour. The toppings are endless, but commonly include pork belly, octopus, squid, prawns or vegetables. Some varieties add a layer of fried noodles, and these are then referred to as modan-yaki, meaning "a lot" or "piled high", signifying the volume of food resulting from having both noodles and Okonomiyaki. In some ways, this dish reminds me of my childhood favourite - "bubble and squeak" - each time you cook it, it turns out different yet delicious!

This dish incorporates a few Japanese ingredients. Most can be sourced from local supermarkets, and if they are not available there, Asian grocery stores will certainly carry them.

1. Enoki mushrooms are highly regarded in Japan for their delicate flavour and crisp texture when eaten raw.

2. Japanese mayonnaise - this egg yolk mayonnaise is often used in sushi.

3. Okonomiyaki sauce, also known as Otafuku, is similar in taste and texture to Worcestershire sauce. It is worth the effort to find this traditional sauce, as it certainly enhances the dish.

4. Bonito flakes are finely shaved dried fish, usually skipjack tuna, which add a distinct umami flavour to the dish.

It is crucial to use a shallow frying pan or flat grill to make these Okonomiyaki. I use my crêpe pan, as it makes flipping the "pancake" during cooking easier. The wider your flipping tool the better - a wide egg slide is ideal. In Japan, a metal slide is used which also serves to cut the pancake for serving.

- 1 cup plain flour
- 330 ml water
- 250 g pork mince
- 4 eggs, beaten
- 170 g cabbage, finely shredded
- 2 spring onions, thinly sliced, whites and green sections separated
- 1 tbl vegetable oil
- 50 g enoki mushrooms

To serve:
- Japanese mayonnaise
- Okonomiyaki sauce
- Bonito flakes

Place the flour in a bowl. Add water and mix until smooth. Cover, and place in the fridge to rest for half an hour.

Meanwhile, heat the oil in a frypan, and brown the pork mince for approximately 5 minutes. Add the whites of the spring onions and cook a further 2 minutes. Turn off the heat and stir through the separated enoki mushrooms.

Add the eggs to the batter and mix well. Stir in the cabbage, ensuring that it is well coated.

Heat a non-stick, shallow frypan or flat skillet. Add ½ cup of batter. Place ¼ of pork mixture on top. Cook for 3-4 minutes until golden brown. Carefully flip the pancake and cook for another 2-3 minutes. Transfer the pancake to a serving plate and repeat with remaining batter making sure you mix the batter well to ensure that all the cabbage is coated each for each pancake.

To serve, sprinkle green spring onions on to each okonomiyaki. Drizzle in a decorative pattern the mayonnaise and okonomiyaki sauce. Top with bonito flakes and enjoy!

https://youtu.be/p8VMT_U6-Dc

Rice paper rolls

Makes 12-14

With the party season heating up, it can be difficult to find a variety of "nibbles" that you can prepare that are gluten-free. Luckily, with Australia being such a multicultural society, the range of ingredients available is enormous and provides endless combinations for your rice paper rolls. Try them with pork, BBQ chicken, coriander, avocado, carrot... the choice is up to you.

These rolls are best eaten straight away. If you do need to store them until the guests arrive, don't put them in the fridge - it just dries them out. Instead, cover them with a damp, clean tea towel.

Traditionally, these are served with hoisin sauce, but they are also great with sweet chilli sauce.

- Rice paper wrappers
- Angel hair noodles (or cellophane noodles)
- Cooked prawns (2 per roll)
- Vietnamese mint
- Shredded lettuce

Dipping Sauce:
- Hoisin sauce
- Crushed peanuts

Prepare noodles according to the packet instructions.

Lay a damp tea towel on your workbench.

Using a flat dish with warm water, gently soak a rice paper wrapper for 3-4 seconds. It will start to soften slightly. Remove from the water and lay onto the tea towel. Place a mint leaf in the centre of the wrapper. Place 2 prawns on the leaf, then add a small amount of each of the remaining ingredients leaving about 5 cm of the wrapper uncovered on each side.

Fold up one side of the wrapper (It will be very soft now, so be careful not to tear it). This forms the bottom of the roll. Do the same with the top of the wrapper, then the left side, then the right side roll tightly to make the shape of the roll. The final join should be placed face down onto the serving plate to help hold the roll together.

Continue with the remaining ingredients.

In a small bowl, combine the hoisin sauce and peanuts.

https://youtu.be/3Z2sqKsGOIU

Tempura mussels

Serves 2

Mussels are a splendid fresh and sustainable source of omega 3, protein, Vitamin B12, selenium, and manganese. They are also low in fat. Mussels are farmed in areas with restricted shipping and regular tidal flows. Here in Victoria, Australia, that means Corio Bay. There are several mussel farmers who operate out of Portarlington, and I've had the privilege of getting to know one of the farmers, Jennifer from Mr Mussel. She has taught me a great deal about these amazing creatures.

I'm incredibly fortunate to have been asked to demonstrate how to cook mussels at the Portarlington Mussel Festival each January. Over the past 11 years, I've shown people how straightforward it is to prepare mussels. For those of you who haven't had the chance to attend my demonstrations, here are my top 5 tips:

1. Fresh mussels can be stored in the fridge for 7-10 days. Keep the mussels covered with a damp tea towel that you replace every 2-3 days.

2. When preparing mussels, allow them to rinse in a sink of cool water for about 10 minutes. This lets them open and release some of the seawater and grit.

3. Debearding a mussel. There's a hard way and an easy way. The hard way - holding the mussel with the pointy end pointing to the sky, grab hold of the beard, and sharply pull it downwards. The easy way - steam the mussels open in an empty pan over medium heat (3-5 minutes). The beards can then be effortlessly removed with a gentle tug. Any juices left in the pan can be strained through a fine mesh strainer and stored in the freezer. This mussel stock is perfect for risottos or paella.

4. Many people believe that any mussels that do not open during cooking need to be discarded and should not be eaten because they're dead! This is TOTALLY INCORRECT. All the mussels in the pan are dead - you've just cooked them! You need to determine if the mussel is no good to eat BEFORE cooking them. There are 2 things to look out for:

a) Discard any with a broken shell. You do not know how long the shell has been broken and the mussel exposed.

b) An open, uncooked mussel is either hungry or unwell. To work out which - tap the mussel on the bench. A hungry, healthy mussel will slowly close up. These can be cooked. Discard any that don't close.

5. When opening cooked mussels that have not opened during the cooking process, use the point of a sharp knife. Be cautious, as the shell will often contain hot water that can scald you.

Tempura batter is a crisp, light batter. It enhances the flavour of the mussel, keeping the meat of the mussel juicy inside the crisp batter casing. These are perfect with a green salad for a light meal, or as an hors d'oeuvre when hosting guests.

The Tempura batter I have used here is made with rice flour, salt, and sugar, and it is gluten-free.

- 1 kg mussels
- ½ cup plain flour
- 1 packet tempura batter mix
- Ice water (as directed on the packet)
- Vegetable oil for frying

Place rinsed mussels in an empty, shallow frypan with a tight-fitting lid. Steam the mussels open over a medium heat.

Debeard the mussels and remove from the shell.

Prepare the tempura batter as per packet instructions.

Lightly coat the mussels in plain flour, shaking to remove excess.

Heat vegetable oil in a deep fryer or wok to between 180-190°C.

Dip the floured mussels into the tempura batter, ensuring all the mussel is coated. Drop into the hot oil and cook for 3-4 minutes. (don't cook more than 6 at a time, otherwise the temperature of the oil will drop and the batter will absorb too much oil and become soggy).

Drain cooked mussels on paper towel.

Serve immediately.

https://youtu.be/p84teAqO6aY

Pomegranate chicken

Serves 3-4

I have to admit that pomegranates were not very common when I was growing up.

My Uncle Alan, affectionately known as "Unc," once drove my brother and I from Melbourne to Adelaide to visit our grandmother during the school holidays. Being a confirmed bachelor at the time, Unc had always embraced the role of jokester uncle with us. This journey was a perfect opportunity for him to unleash a barrage of "dad jokes" on his captive audience as we travelled the eight or so hours across southern Australia. As we passed through Great Western, he spun a tale about "miniature pomegranate trees" lining the road. We had no idea what a pomegranate tree was, let alone a miniature one, we absorbed every detail of the story, eager to share it with Mum and Dad upon our return. Unc initially masked his disappointment that we didn't catch the joke, but he surely relished our retelling of the story to Gramma. That's when she looked quizzically at him and exclaimed, "What! The grapevines!" I was about eight years old during that road trip, and although I didn't encounter my first pomegranate until my thirties, that road trip memory came flooding back vividly.

Pomegranates grow on small trees, originating from the Mediterranean regions. Now, these wonderful fruits are found on every continent except Antarctica. In Australia, the season runs from March to May, and in the northern hemisphere from September to February. They have a tough skin, and inside are segments filled with juicy arils that burst with sweetness. The juice from these arils is the source of grenadine syrup, used to add flavour and colour to various dishes and drinks. Pomegranates are rich in folic acid, vitamins C and K.

This recipe also incorporates pomegranate molasses, a staple ingredient in Mediterranean, Middle Eastern, and North African cooking. It contributes a complex depth to the sweet and tangy nature of the dish. If you're unable to find pomegranate molasses in stores, you can substitute it with more pomegranate juice. Alternatively, if you have time, simmer pomegranate juice over low heat for 90-120 minutes until it reduces to a thick syrup with the consistency of maple syrup. Be careful not to boil the liquid, as this can result in a muddy colour and an overcooked taste.

This dish showcases the wonderful burst of colour and complex flavour of the pomegranate. It's quite quick to prepare and can even be a delightful weeknight dinner.

- 6 chicken thighs with bone
- Salt and pepper, to taste
- 2 tbl olive oil
- 125 ml pomegranate molasses
- 85 ml pomegranate juice
- 2 tbl honey
- 1 tbl balsamic vinegar
- Juice of 1 lemon
- 4 garlic cloves, crushed
- Finely chopped parsley, for garnish
- ½ cup pomegranate seeds

In a flat dish, combine oil, pomegranate molasses, pomegranate juice, honey, vinegar, lemon juice and garlic.

Pat dry chicken pieces and season with salt and pepper.

Place chicken in marinade, turning to coat. Cover and place in the fridge for at least 30 minutes - overnight is fine too.

Preheat oven 200°C fan/220°C.

Place chicken skin side up in an oven proof dish. Pour all of the marinade over the chicken.

Bake for 30 minutes. Increase the oven temperature to 210°C fan/230°C. Brush pieces with the marinade. Bake a further 10 minutes, basting every 5 minutes until the skin goes a golden colour and crispy.

Serves garnished with pomegranate seeds and parsley.

https://youtu.be/lpX73_JhMgE

Chilli and coconut prawns

Serves 2

I'm sure I'm not the only one who sometimes struggles to decide what to cook during the week. A midweek meal needs to be made with ingredients commonly found in the pantry and fridge, be quick to prepare, and still be interesting. Particularly in the warmer months, this recipe ticks all those boxes.

I must reiterate that a rice cooker is almost an essential piece of cooking equipment in your home. This dish is best served with steamed rice. The "set and forget" feature of a rice cooker simplifies the cooking process. Of course, you can also cook rice on the stovetop; if you choose to do so, I recommend using the absorption method.

Now, let's talk about the prawns. Depending on your location and the time of year, the variety of prawns available to you will differ. While there are over 3,000 species of prawns, only 10-15 are commonly consumed. Prawns can be purchased either green (uncooked) or cooked (which are slightly pink in colour). For this recipe, you'll want green prawns that can be marinated to soak up all the wonderful aromatics before being quickly cooked. A great resource for understanding the different types of prawns is available at https://www.taste.com.au/quick-easy/articles/complete-guide-to-prawns/2edybwvn.

I used green prawn cutlets for this dish, prepared by my fishmonger. He removed the head and outer shell, leaving only the flesh and tail, and also deveined the prawns. It's worth noting that prawns aren't always deveined when you buy them. The "vein" is actually the prawn's intestine, and if you need to devein the prawns yourself, here's a handy video link: https://youtu.be/718A8XtADEw.

This recipe is easily scalable. The quantities for the marinade and sauce given here are sufficient for up to 24 prawns, or 4 servings. We prefer to serve it with a generous amount of sauce.

- 12 deveined raw prawn cutlets
- 270 ml coconut cream

Marinade:
- 2 cm fresh ginger, finely chopped into matchsticks
- 2 cloves garlic, chopped
- 2 tbl chopped coriander
- Juice of 2 limes
- 1 tsp turmeric
- 3 tbl vegetable oil
- ½ tsp ground cumin
- 1 cayenne chilli, finely chopped
- 1 tbl brown sugar
- 2 stalks of lemongrass, whites only
- Salt to taste

Combine all marinade ingredients in a medium bowl. Place ½ cup of marinade into a small saucepan and set aside. Place the prawns in a shallow dish and cover with the remainder of the marinade. Toss to make sure all the prawns are coated thoroughly. Cover and chill in the fridge for at least 30 minutes.

Whilst the prawns are marinating prepare your rice in the rice cooker.

To make the sauce add coconut cream to the reserved marinade, and gently heat. Be careful not to boil as the coconut cream will split.

Preheat a griddle or BBQ plate. Cook the prawns for 2-3 minutes on each side.

Serve with steamed rice and spoon over the creamy sauce.

Massaman curry

Serves 4

Australia's multicultural evolution is easy to spot in our food — and nothing tells that story better than curry. In the 1970s, 'curry' meant sausages in a rich sauce made with Keens curry powder, often sweetened with apple or banana to tame the heat. Years later, Myles cooked me a vindaloo — bold, spicy, unforgettable — and it changed how I thought about curry.

Massaman is the gentler cousin: rich with warm spices, sweet and salty layers, and a hit of tamarind for balance. It blends Thai ingredients with Indian flavours and is traditionally made with chicken in Thailand — though beef is more common here.

While store-bought pastes are easy, homemade brings real depth. This recipe makes extra paste, and once you taste it, you'll see why it's worth the effort.

Curry paste:
- 6 dried long red chillies, deseeded
- 1 tsp shrimp paste
- 2 tsp ground coriander
- 2 tsp ground cumin
- 1 tsp ground cinnamon
- ¼ tsp ground cloves
- ½ tsp ground cardamom
- 1 tsp ground white pepper
- 3 shallots, chopped
- 4 cloves garlic, peeled
- 1 stalk lemongrass, white section only (keep green for the curry)
- 1 tsp palm sugar or brown sugar
- 3 cm piece of galangal or ginger, peeled and thinly sliced

Curry:
- 750 g diced beef (chuck steak is best)
- 2 cups beef stock
- ¼ cup vegetable oil
- 400 ml coconut milk
- 1 cinnamon stick
- 1 tsp tamarind paste
- 1 tbl fish sauce
- 6 cocktail potatoes, halved
- 3 tbl peanuts
- 1 lime, cut into wedges

To make the curry paste:

Place chillies in a heatproof bowl. Cover with boiling water. Stand for 20 minutes or until soft. Drain well. Roughly chop.

Wrap shrimp paste in foil. Heat in a frypan over medium heat for 2 to 3 minutes each side or until roasted.

Blend or process chillies, roasted shrimp paste, coriander, cumin, cinnamon, cloves, cardamom, white pepper and 1 tablespoon cold water until smooth. Add remaining ingredients, 1 at a time, blending well after each addition until mixture forms a thick paste.

To make the curry:

Place the beef in a large pot. Add the beef stock and lemongrass green sections. The beef should be almost covered. If not add extra water.

Bring to the boil and then simmer gently for 1.5 hours until beef is very tender.

Remove beef from the pan and set aside. Discard the lemongrass.

Reduce the liquid until you have 375 ml, then set aside.

In a separate pot heat oil. Add 4 tablespoon of curry paste and fry for 2-3 minutes until thick and fragrant. Add coconut milk and stir well.

Add cinnamon stick and reserved beef liquid. Reduce the heat and simmer for 3 minutes.

Stir in fish sauce and tamarind.

Add the potatoes and cook for 7-8 minutes until potatoes are tender.

Add the beef to the pot and simmer for 2-3 minutes. Test for seasoning and adjust as needed. You may add a little water if the sauce is getting too thick.

Remove the cinnamon stick prior to serving over Jasmine rice with scattered peanuts and a lime wedge.

Serve with steamed jasmine rice.

https://youtu.be/wiANguQdUiM

Falafels with tahini sauce

Makes 20

Australia's evolution into a multicultural society has been significantly influenced by food, serving as a gateway for new migrants. It's fascinating to consider that Melbourne, now renowned as the coffee capital of the world, didn't see its first espresso machine until 1928 and only developed a café culture in the 1950s. Initially, new cuisines were slow to gain acceptance, but now, Melbourne boasts a rich tapestry of culinary fusions from various food cultures.

In this vibrant culinary landscape, the falafel, a staple of Middle Eastern cuisine, remains unchanged. It's ubiquitous across Melbourne, found in street stalls, food trucks, cafés, and bars, and embraced as a snack, breakfast, or lunch option throughout the city and beyond.

Falafels, naturally gluten-free, are a personal favourite of mine. The ideal falafel is served warm, with a crispy exterior and a light, fluffy interior, complemented by tahini sauce. There's some debate about the necessity of baking powder in falafel recipes, but I firmly believe it's essential. Without baking powder, falafels can turn out dense, but with it, they achieve a desirable light and fluffy texture.

Chickpeas, the primary ingredient in falafels, are a legume rich in protein and fibre and have a low glycemic index (GI). This means they're not only nutritious but also provide a steady energy release. For making falafels, it's crucial to use dried chickpeas soaked in cold water for at least eight hours, allowing them to double in size. Tinned chickpeas, while great for hummus, are unsuitable for falafels due to their pre-cooked nature. If you forget to soak the chickpeas overnight, there are quick-soak methods available, as outlined at https://www.thespruceeats.com/soak-and-cook-dried-chickpeas-2356061.

Falafels are versatile, making a perfect snack served with tahini sauce, a delightful breakfast paired with a poached egg, or a satisfying lunch stuffed into pita bread with salad.

- 225 g dried chickpeas - soaked overnight
- 1 cup flat parsley leaves (20 g)
- 1 cup coriander leaves (20 g)
- 1 small brown onion, chopped
- 2 cloves of garlic, sliced
- 1 tsp cumin
- ½ tsp ground coriander
- 1½ tsp salt
- ½ tsp baking powder
- 4 tsp chickpea flour
- 2 tbl cold water

Vegetable oil for frying

Tahini sauce
- 4 tbl tahini
- 2 tbl lemon juice
- 4 tbl cold water
- ¼ tsp salt

Drain chickpeas and place in a food processor. Add parsley, coriander, onion, garlic, cumin, ground coriander, salt, baking powder, chickpea flour and water. Pulse for 3-4 minutes until fine.

Using a small scoop or spoon make into balls and place onto a lined tray.

Refrigerate for 30 minutes.

Pour oil into a large pot - at least 2cm deep. Heat on medium high to 180 - 190°C.

Place a ball in a large spoon and carefully slide ball into the oil. Cook in batches for around 2-3 minutes, until deep golden and super crusty on the outside.

Drain on paper towel.

Tahini sauce:

Combine tahini and lemon juice, and mix well. The mixture will stiffen.

Stir in the water 1 tablespoon at a time and it will loosen again. The final consistency should be like a thick drizzle sauce

Season to taste with salt.

The Phoenician Table

Home isn't always where you live.

Some places pull at your heartstrings and feel familiar and comfortable the minute you step off the plane. For me, the Mediterranean is that place. My roots are here, and every time I visit, I learn more about who I am and where I come from.

The Phoenician empire was situated on the east coast of the Mediterranean, in what today is known as Lebanon. As great traders, their routes extended to modern-day Egypt, Sicily, Malta, Tripoli, Morocco, and Malaga in Spain. They traded in fine goods, oils, timber, and spices.

For the Phoenicians, the eye was a symbol of protection and good health, so eyes were painted onto their boats to protect fishermen and traders from harm while at sea. In the port of Marsaxlokk in Malta, these colourful symbols of history and continuity can still be seen today.

My dad was a fabulous cook.

Many of the dishes in this chapter I learned from him. He was born in Hamrun on the island of Malta in 1932. The impact of WWII could be seen in many aspects of his life. Food was never wasted; grow whatever you can and barter for the things you didn't grow; share food with family always. As with many parts of the Phoenician empire, shared plates, lots of variety with colour and spices, good olives, and crusty bread were shared with laughter and love.

Traditional Maltese luzzu boats in Marsaxlokk

Dark chocolate florentines

Makes 12

Christmas time is a significant milestone on the calendar. For many, it's an opportunity to reconnect with friends and family, often accompanied by the tradition of gift-giving.

According to historical records, the act of giving gifts has been around since antiquity. As Homer outlined, the duty of kindness and generosity towards others served as a force for social good. The widespread practice of gift-giving across diverse cultures, religions, and languages suggests that it's fundamental to the human condition. (https://thegiftcollective.com/blog/a-short-history-of-gift-giving)

Different families have various ways of managing this tradition. These range from using a Kris Kringle system to pooling resources for a larger gift. While it's often joyful, gift-giving can also be stressful. Concerns about the appropriateness, size, and cost of gifts abound. Retailers start advertising for Christmas as early as October, enticing us with "perfect gift ideas," many of which are items we didn't even know existed.

For me, the real joy is in the giving – particularly when it results in a smile from a loved one. And who wouldn't smile at a gift made with love and chocolate?

These treats are easy to make and store well in an airtight container. The ingredients are also flexible; you can mix-and-match fruits and nuts to match your personal taste, pantry, and budget. I've opted for combinations that evoke the Christmas colours of red and green.

- 100 g slivered almonds
- 70 g shelled pistachios
- 35 g glacé cherries, chopped
- 35 g dried cranberries
- ½ tsp orange zest
- 45 g unsalted butter
- 60 g sugar
- 1 tbl honey
- 15 g plain flour (GF)
- 75 g 70% dark chocolate
- Butter, for greasing the tin

- 12 strips of baking paper, each 2cm wide x 10cm long

Preheat oven to 160°C fan/180°C.

Grease a 12-hole non-stick muffin tin with butter. Place a strip of baking paper in each hole with both ends sticking out the top.

In a large bowl place almonds, pistachios, cherries, cranberries and orange zest and mix well.

In a small saucepan over a low heat, mix together butter, honey, sugar and flour until the sugar dissolves and butter has melted.

Pour the butter mixture over the fruit and nuts in the bowl and mix well until everything is well coated.

Dollop heaped dessert spoons of mixture into each hole of the tin.

Bake 15-20 minutes until golden. You may need to turn your tray around at the 15-minute mark.

Allow to cool completely in the tin. Then use the paper strip to gently lift them out.

Break up the chocolate into a heatproof bowl and melt in the microwave (approx. 90 seconds, but check after 1 minute). Dip the base of the biscuits in the chocolate and place chocolate side up on a baking tray. Place in the fridge for 15 minutes to set.

https://youtu.be/POBDP5iMX4I

Italian ricotta donuts (Frittelle Di Ricotta)

Makes 20

Who can resist the delicious aroma of a doughnut? As a child, I preferred mine hot, dusted in cinnamon sugar, or oozing with rich raspberry jam. But as I have grown older, my tastes have changed. These doughnuts are very grown up and sophisticated, yet surprisingly simple to make.

Warning: you won't want to stop at one!

In Italian they are called Frittelle, and are bite-sized morsels, light and crunchy on the outside, smooth and creamy on the inside. They were surprisingly easy to convert to gluten-free by adding baking powder and using a standard gluten-free flour mix.

Prosecco is an Italian sparkling wine. It adds lightness to the batter.

These are best served immediately, but as they only take 2-3 minutes to cook, your guests won't be waiting too long. As with all gluten-free, the batter is best cooked straight away. It too, is quick to prepare.

When deep-frying, I use a wok because it is easy to handle and deep enough. Your oil should be 175°C - 190°C before starting to cook. If you don't have a food thermometer, drop a small amount of batter into the oil - if there isn't any bubbling then the oil isn't ready. If it is furiously bubbling and smoking then the oil is too hot. Be careful not to overcrowd the pan as it will drop the temperature of the oil and you will get soggy, oily donuts.

- 2 eggs, lightly beaten
- 1 tbl sugar
- 250 g fresh ricotta
- Fine zest of 1 orange
- 120 g self-raising flour (GF)
- 1 tsp baking powder (GF)
- Pinch of salt
- 150 ml Prosecco
- Olive oil for deep frying
- Icing sugar for dusting
- Coarse orange zest for garnish

Combine eggs, ricotta, sugar, salt and orange zest in a large bowl. Mix until smooth.

Add the flour, baking powder and prosecco. Mix lightly until just combined - a few lumps add to the texture.

Heat oil in a wok until 175°C - 190°C. Drop tablespoons of batter into the oil - usually 3-4 at a time so as not to overcrowd the oil. Turn gently until golden brown - 2-3 minutes.

Drain on paper towel.

To serve, dust with icing sugar and orange zest.

https://youtu.be/YkRwh9-n4go

Panna cotta with roasted peaches

Serves 6

There are many memories of childhood summers - squeals as you ran under the sprinkler, icy-poles melting down your hands as they melted faster than you could eat them. But the smell of ripe peaches always evokes the feelings of carefree, endless summers of childhood. We had a giant peach tree behind our garage, the white variety. Nothing beats the taste of a ripe peach as you bite into it and have the juices running down your chin.

Sadly, I no longer have a peach tree, although my friend Rhonda has a magnificent yellow freestone tree that she shares her bounty with us - these I bottle to enjoy in the depths of winter, when summer feels a long way away.

So as summer is coming to an end, this dish evokes all those memories. In my YouTube video, I have served the peaches in a glass where the pannacotta has been set on an angle. This is very suitable for a dinner party and also means there is no need to unmould the panna cotta. The peach skin is a little tough when cooked, so you may wish to cut the fruit into smaller pieces. The skin does help the fruit maintain its shape during cooking. For us, I usually make the panna cotta in 150 ml moulds, which I then run under hot water for a few seconds before turning out onto a cold plate. Then I leave the peaches in halves to roast and fill the centre hole where the stone was, with the toasted almonds.

Don't skip the mint - even though you will use only a few leaves, the mint makes this dessert pop!

- 300 ml cream
- 300 ml milk
- ¼ cup castor sugar
- 1 vanilla pod, split
- 4 gelatine leaves

- 3 peaches
- 2 tsp honey
- ¼ tsp lemon zest
- 2 tbl brown sugar
- 10 g butter
- 2 tsp water
- 1 tbl brandy (optional)
- ½ tsp vanilla extract

To serve
- Mint
- ¼ cup slivered almonds, toasted

Panna cotta (make ahead)

In a large saucepan, gently heat the milk, cream, and sugar until it reaches 40 degrees. Take from the heat and add the vanilla pod. Allow to sit for 10 minutes to infuse.

Soak the gelatine leaves in cold water.

Remove the vanilla pod and heat on high until 90 degrees (just before boiling). Remove from the heat and stir in the gelatine leaves one at a time.

Lay 6 glasses at a 45-degree slant and carefully pour in the custard. Refrigerate for 4 hours.

Roasted Peaches

Preheat oven 220°C fan/240°C.

Halve the peaches and remove the stones. Cut each half into 4.

Arrange the fruit in a small baking dish. Sprinkle with brown sugar and lemon zest. Mix together the vanilla, brandy, and water and pour over the peaches. Drizzle with honey. Dob small pieces of butter onto each piece of fruit.

Bake for 20 minutes, basting at the 10-minute mark, until caramelised.

Set aside to come to room temperature.

To toast the almonds, place them in a hot, dry pan and stir constantly until golden. Remove from the pan and allow to cool.

To Serve

Carefully place 4 pieces of peach in each glass. Sprinkle with toasted slivered almonds and finely shredded mint leaves.

https://youtu.be/7d-F6rCSW5Y

Bragioli (Beef olives)

Makes 6

Bragioli, or Beef Olives, are a traditional Maltese dish — one of the few naturally gluten-free Maltese recipes. Regular readers of my blog may recall that in 2014, I posted an "in memory" tribute to my dad, who passed away on March 23rd that year. He was a passionate cook of traditional Maltese dishes. I cooked these to honour him, even though we rarely made them at home, as we often had them at my Uncle Romeo's, where Aunty Mary made exceptional Bragioli.

It should be noted that this recipe contains no olives! The name refers to the oval shape of the meat and the fact that it's stuffed, like an olive.

Each time I travel to Malta, we dine with the Sisters of the Sacred Heart community, where my Auntie Juliet resides — a special treat full of great food and intriguing conversation. Myles often seizes the chance to pose theological questions to Mother Superior, given his non-religious upbringing. The combination of food and conversation makes this meal a trip highlight.

Auntie Juliet often prepares Bragioli for us — ideal for sharing with family or guests. Served hot with mashed potatoes and vegetables, or cold in sandwiches or with salad, they're perfect any way you serve them.

Sauce:
- 3 tbl olive oil
- 2 large onions, diced
- 5 garlic cloves, crushed
- 400 g tin of tomatoes
- 1 cup flat-leaf parsley, roughly chopped
- 2 bay leaves
- 250 ml red wine
- 500 ml water
- Salt and pepper, to taste

Beef olives:
- 6 thin slices of topside, weiner schnitzel, or round steak
- 6 boiled eggs, shells removed
- 400 g minced veal or pork
- 2 bacon rashers, diced
- 2 garlic cloves, crushed
- ½ cup flat-leaf parsley, finely chopped
- 1 tbl chopped fresh oregano
- 1 spring onion, sliced
- ½ cup gbejniet (Maltese cheese) (optional)
- 2 eggs, beaten

Heat oil in a solid-based, large saucepan. Add onion and garlic and cook until translucent. Add the remaining sauce ingredients and simmer whilst making the beef olives.

Flatten the beef slices with a meat mallet. Trim the edges. Put aside.

Mix all remaining ingredients together, seasoning well with salt and pepper. Place a generous spoonful of mixture onto each slice of beef and spread it out well. Place a boiled egg in the centre, and roll up and secure with toothpicks.

Place in the simmering sauce and simmer for 90 minutes over low heat. You may need to add extra water to the sauce to stop it drying out.

https://youtu.be/d9q8TsVjfag

Chicken cacciatore

Serves 2-3

Chicken Cacciatore is a fantastic winter warmer that's perfect for feeding a crowd. There are probably as many recipes for this dish as there are nonnas! My introduction to it didn't come from any of my Maltese relatives, but from a cookbook I received when I was about 10, aptly titled "My First Cookbook". This gem of a book includes culinary classics like eggman salad, baked bean hotpot, pineapple upside-down cake and chicken cacciatore. Even though the version I whip up today has evolved considerably from the one in that childhood cookbook, its influence on my current rendition is undeniable.

Over the years, I've incorporated several adaptations and nuances to my version of this comforting dish. For instance, I've developed a fondness for the briny sharpness that capers add to the rich tomato sauce. I've also introduced red wine into the mix, lending a deeper, more robust flavour to the sauce and enhancing the complexity of the dish. The resultant recipe, while differing from the original, remains true to the spirit of Chicken Cacciatore - a hearty, satisfying meal that brings warmth and joy to any dining table.

- 3 chicken Maryland pieces
- 20 g capers
- 250 ml red wine
- 100 g black olives
- 1 can of tomatoes
- 1 onion, finely chopped
- 1 carrot, diced
- 2 cloves of garlic, finely sliced
- 3 tbl olive oil

Preheat oven to 180°C fan/200°C.

Heat olive oil in a heavy-based pot. Place chicken in the pot and fry until skin is golden all over. Remove chicken from pot. Gently fry onion until translucent.

Return chicken to the pot and add remaining ingredients. Cover and place in the oven for 30 minutes. Check fluid level, you may need to add a cup of water or red wine to prevent the chicken from drying out. Cook for another 30 minutes.

Serve with freshly cooked pasta, cooked soft polenta or creamy mashed potatoes and crusty bread.

Chicken tagine and jewelled rice

Serves 4

A taste of Morocco: For those who know me, it is probably no surprise when I say: I LOVE hats. I am rarely seen without one and often find them in wonderful markets around the world or designed by my milliner. So, what did this have to do with a Moroccan dish like Chicken Tagine with preserved lemon? To celebrate my 50th birthday, I bought a Fez from Fes. The trip became a reality—Marrakesh's markets, intricate mosaics, the romance of Casablanca, and of course, the hat shops of Fes.

Tagines originated in Berber culture and are used throughout North Africa to cook meat, chicken or fish with dried fruits, spices and nuts. I've used a traditional earthenware tagine, but a saucepan with a tight lid works too. The conical lid shape helps steam condense and return to the pot, keeping everything moist and full of flavour. Tagines can be used on the stovetop or in the oven. For stovetop cooking, use the lowest heat and a diffuser to spread heat evenly. Some tagines are beautifully decorated—these are for serving, not cooking.

Tagine:
- 8 chicken thighs, bone-in
- 2 chicken livers (optional)
- 2 tsp salt
- 1 tsp ground ginger
- 1 tsp paprika
- ¼ tsp cumin
- 1 onion, grated
- 1 pinch saffron threads
- 150 g green olives
- ¼ preserved lemon, flesh discarded and rind sliced thinly
- Juice of 1 lemon
- Chopped coriander and parsley for garnish

Jewelled rice:
- 2 pinches saffron threads
- ¼ cup boiling water
- 2 cups basmati rice
- 2 tbl olive oil
- ¾ cup dried cranberries
- ½ cup currants
- ½ cup dried apricots, finely sliced
- Zest of 2 oranges
- ¼ cup slivered almonds
- ¼ cup pistachios, roughly chopped

Heat a small amount of olive oil in the base of the tagine. Gently fry the onion and chicken livers (if using) until livers are still pink in the middle and onion is just starting to colour. Remove from tagine and keep aside.

In batches, fry the chicken pieces until browned all over, putting aside on a plate until all chicken is browned and removed from tagine. Add salt, ginger, paprika, cumin and saffron to the tagine and fry until fragrant. Return the chicken to the tagine, rolling in the spice mix as you go. Add the preserved lemon. Pour over the lemon juice and cover. Cook on a gently simmer for 30 minutes until chicken is cooked.

In the meantime, mash the livers with a fork to form a paste.

When chicken juices run clear when pricked with a fork, remove chicken from the tagine. Return chicken livers and onion to the tagine and stir though the liquid, allowing sauce to thicken slightly. Add olives to the tagine and stir through. Place chicken on top of olives, replace the lid and cook for a further 5-10 minutes to heat through.

Serve with garnish of chopped parsley and coriander.

To prepare the rice:

Rinse rice well in cold water, until water runs clear. Add to a pot of boiling water and simmer for 10 minutes. Drain well.

Add boiling water to saffron and allow to steep.

Heat a large, heavy based saucepan. Add olive oil. Add drained, hot rice and toss through. Add saffron, including the liquid and stir through well. Stir in all remaining ingredients.

Cover with a lid, and leave on the lowest heat for 5-8 minutes.

Fluff with a fork to serve.

https://youtu.be/DdxxlhelkQM

Imqarrun il-forn (Maltese baked pasta)

Serves 4

This recipe triggers a strong emotional response for me. In Malta, this traditional dish can be found in every home and corner bakery. Given its ubiquity, there are naturally many variations. The one I'm sharing is my Dad's!

In Australia during the 1970s, our food vocabulary for dishes from outside Britain was fairly limited. Most Aussies referred to any type of pasta simply as "spaghetti"—often from a tin. My Australian family was no different. So, when Dad first served this dish at a family meal, there was a lot of apprehension from the guests. Within the family, it became known as "baked spaghetti." Everyone was quickly won over by the crunchy top. My Uncle Andy and Aunt Carol would hang around the kitchen at serving time just to snaffle the best bits before they made it to the table. It took immense willpower while filming this dish not to snatch a crunchy piece before we'd finished taking photos!

In my family, we like the pasta's top extra crunchy, bordering on almost burnt—though it's not actually burnt, so don't be fooled! You do have to be careful not to genuinely burn it.

For the meat, I've used a combination of beef and pork mince. Many Maltese opt for canned corned beef, likely a holdover from WWII when tinned meat was a mainstay. Dad's version uses beaten eggs, but some in my Maltese family prefer hard-boiled eggs chopped through the dish. I find the beaten eggs add a creamy texture to the sauce that I really enjoy.

Now, let's talk about the pasta. Dad always used bucatini, a thick spaghetti-like pasta with a hole through its centre. It's not easy to find in Australia, especially a gluten-free version. Both penne and rigatoni make good substitutes—their tubes and ridges are perfect for holding sauce. Dried pasta works best. I've tried using homemade penne, but it's too soft and doesn't hold up to the double-cooking method. I use an Italian made gluten-free penne as it's robust and holds its shape well, even when reheating leftovers.

This dish can easily be adapted into another famous Maltese dish called Timpana by encasing the filling in a pie crust. Personally, I prefer it with the crunchy top.

- Olive oil
- 250 g pork mince
- 250 g beef mince
- 1 brown onion, diced
- 2 cloves garlic, finely chopped
- 2 tbl tomato paste (Maltese kunserva)
- 1 400 g can crushed tomatoes (or 300 ml passata)
- 1 tsp sugar
- 2 bay leaves
- 2 tsp mixed dried herbs
- 2 large eggs, lightly beaten
- Salt and pepper
- 1 cup grated tasty cheese
- 200 g grated parmesan
- 500 g penne or rigatoni pasta

In a large frypan, heat olive oil and fry the onion until translucent. Add garlic and cook for another minute.

Add mixed herbs and tomato paste, and cook for about 3 minutes.

Add the combined minced meat and cook until browned. Season with salt, pepper and sugar.

Stir in crushed tomatoes, a can of water, and bay leaves. Bring to a gentle simmer. Cover and simmer on low for 30 minutes, stirring occasionally to prevent sticking.

Preheat oven to 180°C fan/200°C.

While the sauce simmers, boil a pot of salted water. Add pasta and cook a minute or two less than packet instructions — it should be al dente. Strain and return to the pot.

Remove bay leaves from the sauce. Spoon a little into a baking dish to stop the pasta sticking.

Remove sauce from the heat and stir in beaten eggs, mixing gently to avoid streaks.

In a small bowl, combine the two cheeses.

Add sauce to the pasta along with a large handful of cheese and mix gently to coat.

Transfer to the baking dish and press down gently. Top with grated cheese and a sprinkle of black pepper.

Bake on the middle rack for 45 minutes. Let rest a few minutes before slicing to help it set.

https://youtu.be/FpToLnQ2ASw

Lasagne

Serves 4

On cold winter nights, there's nothing quite like sitting down to a plate of piping hot lasagne. This is my go-to "brain dead" meal — easy to throw together, and I always have the ingredients on hand. It's also incredibly simple to convert to gluten-free — just use gluten free pasta and plain flour.

In this recipe, I've used dried lasagne sheets. They're convenient to store in the cupboard, especially handy on weeknights. On weekends, I typically use homemade pasta sheets. While this adds about 45 minutes, my family — somewhat disappointingly — often can't tell the difference!

The secret to exceptional lasagne lies in the meat sauce. It should be rich, thick, and full of flavour. Mine includes chili, garlic, mushrooms, and spinach. Of course, these are optional depending on your family's tastes.

To help the lasagne slices hold their shape when served, a little béchamel sauce is needed in each layer. My high school friend's mum, Mrs. Gatto, whose lasagne was unbelievably good, showed me a secret. We weren't allowed in the kitchen while she made the meat sauce — but we could watch her assemble it.

- 1 tbl olive oil
- 1 brown onion, diced
- 1 clove garlic, minced
- 1 chilli, finely sliced (optional)
- 500 g beef mince
- 250 g mushrooms, finely sliced
- 400 g tin diced tomatoes
- 140 g tomato paste
- 1 cup red wine (optional)
- 2 bay leaves
- 1 tbl fresh herbs, finely chopped (e.g. thyme, basil, parsley)
- Salt and pepper, to taste
- 500 ml water
- 100 g spinach leaves (optional)
- 1 packet of lasagne sheets

Béchamel sauce:
- 60 g butter
- Salt and pepper, to taste
- 60 g plain flour
- 600 ml milk
- 150 g tasty cheese, grated

Preheat oven to 190°C fan/210°C.

Heat oil in a large frypan. Add onion, garlic and chilli and gently fry until onions start to soften. Add mince and stir constantly, breaking up lumps of meat, until the meat is well browned.

Add mushrooms, tomatoes, tomato paste, wine, bay leaves, herbs, salt and pepper and stir well. Add water, cover and bring to a gentle simmer for 20 minutes.

Remove bay leaves.

Béchamel sauce:

In a medium saucepan melt butter. Season with salt and pepper.

Add flour, continuing on gentle heat to mix, until the mixture forms a roux and comes away from the sides of the pot.

Slowly add the milk, mixing well between additions to remove any lumps.

Assemble lasagne:

Spoon some of the meat sauce into a rectangular baking dish. Spread to cover dish. This prevents the lasagne from sticking to the bottom.

Place one layer of pasta sheets, then spoon on ⅓ of the meat sauce. Add a layer of spinach leaves. Then spoon two tablespoons of the béchamel sauce across the dish (this helps hold the lasagne together). Repeat these layers until all the meat sauce has been used. The final layer consists of a layer of pasta, which is then covered with a layer of béchamel sauce. Generously cover with grated cheese.

Bake in the oven for 40 minutes.

Serve with crusty bread.

Gnocchi with burnt butter, sage, and gorgonzola

Serves 2

There is something very comforting about sitting down to a large bowl of steaming gnocchi. It is also a very easy recipe to convert to gluten-free, just by substituting in a commercially produced gluten-free plain flour.

There are many variations of gnocchi - some made with semolina or breadcrumbs. There is also much debate as to whether egg should be included. I find that gnocchi made with egg are heavier.

There are a few key tricks -

1. Use starchy potatoes. I prefer Desiree.

2. Boil the potatoes in their skins, or steam them. This is to prevent the flesh getting waterlogged, reducing the flour required.

3. Use a mouli or ricer to mash the potatoes. DO NOT use a food processor as it activates the starch and makes the gnocchi heavy.

4. Work with the potatoes warm - this reduces the amount of flour used.

5. Always have your sauce ready BEFORE cooking the gnocchi.

Most recipes suggest that you use the back of a fork to make the ridges that help the sauce coat the little pillows of gnocchi. You can also use a butter pat or a gnocchi board. They also taste just fine without any ridges at all!

- 1 kg potatoes
- 300 g plain flour
- Salt

Sauce:
- 150 g butter
- Fresh sage leaves
- 100 g gorgonzola cheese

Boil whole, unpeeled potatoes until tender (15-20 minutes depending on their size). Drain and allow to cool until you are able to hold them. Peel potatoes. Using a mouli or ricer, mash the potatoes finely directly onto the bench. Sprinkle with salt.

Work in about half of the flour using the heel of your hand. Keep adding flour until the flour is incorporated and the dough is not too sticky. The faster you do this, the lighter the gnocchi.

Roll dough into a long sausage, about the diameter of your thumb. Cut into 1-2 cm sized pieces.

Roll each piece over the back of a fork, or across a gnocchi board to add the ridges.

Bring a large pot of salted water to the boil. Adjust to a simmer and then gently add the gnocchi. As they rise to the surface drain and serve with your favourite sauce.

Whilst the water is coming the boil, gently melt the butter until browned. Add sage leaves. When the gnocchi is cooking, add the gorgonzola to the butter and stir gently to melt it.

To finish, add the drained gnocchi to the sauce and toss to coat each morsel.

Mushroom arancini with goats cheese

Makes 14 (80 g balls)

Since being diagnosed with coeliac disease, arancini have been a café delicacy I've sorely missed. Paired with a salad, they're perfect for a light meal. Most ingredients are naturally gluten-free—until you hit that fabulous crunchy coating. But let's not get ahead of ourselves.

Arancini are a mouth-watering, multicultural snack that's stood the test of time. They originated in Sicily around the 10th century as portable rice balls for travellers, with fillings evolving over time. Today, they come in round or cone shapes, often filled with ragu or cheese, and remain a beloved part of Sicilian cuisine. The cone-shaped ones pay homage to the magnificent Mount Etna in eastern Sicily, while the round balls are named for their size, akin to a small orange (arancia means "orange" in Italian).

Last year, my niece Grace challenged me to cut down on meat and add vegetarian days to our week. Goat's cheese and mushrooms proved a winning combination in this dish.

The secret to gluten-free success is the crisp coating. Panko crumbs—made from steamed, crustless bread then flaked and dried—are ideal. Their large, airy flakes keep food crisp and absorb less fat. Gluten-free panko, available at specialist and some larger supermarkets (Orgran brand is common in Australia), works best. If unavailable, use gluten-free dried breadcrumbs.

Arancini are worth making in bulk—they freeze well for up to two months once fried. To reheat, bake from frozen at 190°C fan/210°C for 20 minutes. An arancini mould helps with larger batches. I use an 80g mould purchased from Italian cooking suppliers—available in both round and cone shapes, also in 160g sizes.

Arancini even have their own celebration: December 13th, the feast of St Lucia. On this day, bread and pasta are avoided, so arancini are served to mark the occasion.

- 60 g butter
- 1 tbl olive oil
- 1 shallot, finely diced
- 2 cups arborio rice
- 1 l vegetable stock
- 300 g Swiss brown mushrooms, finely diced
- 100 g Parmesan, grated
- 200 g goat cheese, cut into 14 pieces

Coating:
- 100 g plain flour (GF)
- 180 ml water
- 2 eggs
- 350 g panko breadcrumbs (GF)

- Sunflower oil for frying

In a large saucepan, melt the butter with the olive oil. Add the shallot and gently fry until translucent. Add the rice and stir. Cook for 1-2 minutes. Add the mushrooms and mix well. Gradually add the stock, stirring well after each addition until well absorbed. Continue until rice is cooked but al dente (approx 20 minutes). Stir through parmesan. Spread cooked rice onto a cold tray to cool until lukewarm / room temperature.

Once rice is at room temperature, form rice balls with wet hands, using a heaped ice cream scoop of rice for each. Alternatively use an arancini mould. Stuff each rice ball with a cube of goat's cheese and form a tight ball to enclose the cheese. Continue until 14 are made.

To crumb

In a medium-sized bowl beat together the water, flour and eggs.

Place the panko crumbs on a plate.

Dip each ball into the egg mixture and then roll in the panko crumbs until evenly coated.

Heat oil to 190°C. Toss in a breadcrumb and if it starts sizzling immediately, the oil is hot enough. Gently immerse the arancini in the oil, until golden brown 3-4 minutes. Don't overcrowd the pan as it drops the temperature of the oil. Drain on absorbent paper. Repeat with remaining balls.

Great served with a salad and tomato chutney.

https://youtu.be/EolrP8cAc2E

Shakshuka (Baked eggs)

Serves 2

Pronounced Shak-SHOO-kah, this dish is a vibrant reflection of its Middle Eastern and North African roots. Shakshuka, meaning "a mixture" or "shaken" in Arabic, consists of softly cooked eggs, gently poached or braised in a hearty chunky tomato sauce. It's versatile, allowing for a vegetarian serving or the addition of meats like chorizo, speck, or even leftover roast lamb. True to its name, it's a dish that invites creativity with whatever ingredients are on hand. While commonly served for breakfast, it's perfectly suited for any meal.

When I serve Shakshuka for a lazy Sunday brunch, I love to crumble marinated goat's feta over the top before baking. This salty, creamy addition elevates the dish beautifully.

There's no definitive way to serve this delightful dish, but in my opinion bread is a must-have accompaniment. Shakshuka can be prepared on the stovetop, over a campfire, or in the oven. It's adaptable for individual servings or made in a large pan to feed a group, making it wonderfully scalable.

- 200 g (½ can) crushed tomatoes
- ½ red onion, finely sliced
- 1 small clove garlic, minced
- 50 g red capsicum, finely diced
- 2 button mushrooms, finely diced
- ½ tomato, diced
- 125 g cannellini beans, drained and rinsed (½ can)
- 2 tsp tomato paste
- 125 ml water
- ½ tsp smoked paprika
- 1 tsp cumin
- 1 pinch cayenne pepper
- ¼ tsp black pepper
- ½ tsp salt
- 2 eggs
- 2 tbl finely chopped parsley, to serve
- Crusty bread

Preheat oven to 190°C fan/210°C.

In a large frypan, heat the oil. Add the garlic and onion and cook until soft. Add the capsicum and mushroom and cook for 1 minute, then add the fresh tomato and cook another minute.

Add the canned tomatoes, beans, tomato paste, water, paprika, cumin, pepper, cayenne and salt. Stir gently so as not to break up the beans. Cook for 5 minutes until just thick enough to make indentations.

If making individual serves, transfer into oven proof wide ramekins.

Using a large spoon, make an indentation in the sauce and crack in the eggs.

Place in the oven for 10-15 minutes until the whites are set and the yolks runny (or 20-25 if you want very cooked eggs).

Remove from the oven and sprinkle with parsley.

Serve immediately with crusty bread.

https://youtu.be/mvPCtwCkz0E

Moroccan lamb kefta tagine

Serves 4

Morocco is everything you imagine and a total surprise! It's wonderful. The colour; the noise of the markets - motorbikes and donkeys; the aroma of bread being cooked on open fires; the spice markets; the tagines; the amazing craftsmen; the souks (covered markets) - I loved it all and would love to return again.

As both bread and couscous are staple foods in Morocco, my menu choices were at times a little restricted due to coeliac disease. The incredible range of olives, goat's cheeses, salads, amazing oranges, and dates meant I never went hungry.

One meal I had often on my trip to Morocco was a kefta tagine. Although each dish was similar - meatballs in a tomato sauce, often with a poached egg, each was subtly different with a range of spices used. They were cooked and served in an individual portion in restaurants and cafes, but at home, the cooking was done in a large tagine.

Tagines are a traditional Berber cooking implement from North Africa. Most often made from earthenware, they are designed to be cooked over an open fire. In most cases where I saw them being used, they were placed on an earthenware stand on a gas burner. This is to protect the base of the tagine and prevent it from cracking. When cooking at home, I use a diffuser to protect the base from the direct flames.

The cone-shaped lid allows the steam to condense and return to the pot, keeping the dish moist and delicious. This is especially important when cooking chicken dishes, as the majority of chicken eaten is skinless - but that's a story for another day.

If you don't have a tagine, you can cook this dish in a large frying pan with a lid.

- 700 g minced lamb
- 1 onion, finely chopped
- 2 cloves garlic, minced
- 2 tbl finely chopped fresh parsley
- ½ tsp cayenne pepper
- ½ tsp ground ginger
- 1 tsp ground cumin
- 1 tsp paprika
- Olive oil

Sauce:

- 1 onion, chopped
- 2 cloves garlic, finely sliced
- 2 tsp ground cumin
- ½ tsp ground cinnamon
- 1 tsp paprika
- 800 g tin diced tomatoes
- 2 tbl finely chopped fresh parsley
- 4 eggs

Combine lamb, onion, garlic, parsley and spices in a large bowl. Roll mixture into walnut-sized balls.

Heat the oil in the tagine, and cook the meatballs in batches until browned all over. Remove meatballs and set aside.

Add the onion to the tagine and a little more oil if required. Cook until onion is soft. Add garlic and spices. Cook for 30 seconds. Stir in the tomatoes and bring to a simmer. Cook for 15 minutes to allow the flavours to develop.

Add the meatballs back into the tagine, and cook for 10 minutes until cooked. Carefully add the eggs. Cover and cook for 3 minutes until the eggs are poached.

Sprinkle with parsley and serve with crusty bread to soak up the juices.

https://youtu.be/i00Jmpky2EU

Prosciutto wrapped beef with mushrooms

Serves 6

Christmas time for our family is a chance to reconnect, wind down, share stories and create memories. Sometimes the feasts are quite low-key—a barbecue, a cheese platter, or a few Christmas nibbles like mince pies or shortbread. On other occasions, the food is far more elaborate, often with each individual bringing their signature dish. This dish became one of my signatures quite by accident.

About 15 years ago, Aunt Bev and Uncle Geoff hosted the Abbott family Christmas. I was asked to bring the baked ham. I was at work on the Saturday, so Myles went to my butcher to collect the ham on the bone that I had ordered. Disaster struck — the butcher's order of hams hadn't arrived. Instead, Myles was offered a Girello roast. When I came home and went to cook the ham, I found something entirely different in the fridge. In Myles' defence, the butcher had assured him it was a superior cut of meat and that I'd know exactly what to do with it!

Fortunately, I'd recently read Jamie Oliver's "The Return of the Naked Chef", and his recipe sprang to mind. With no time to shop for ingredients, I had to improvise with what I had on hand. Despite initial disappointment over the missing ham, the family loved the dish, and it has since become a Christmas staple. Everyone has their favourite part — be it the crispy, salty prosciutto, the buttery mushrooms, or the tender slice of beef.

Let's discuss the cut of beef. I use a Girello roast because it holds its shape well and is easy to find at my local butcher. Girello is Aussie or Italian for what's called Eye of Round Beef in the US. It's a cut that has little to no fat marbling, making it unsuitable for low-and-slow cooking. When roasting, don't overcook it; serve it medium-rare to medium, or else it will be dry. https://www.glentorriepastures.com/recipes/girello-quick-lean-and-delicious

The prosciutto shouldn't be too thin, or it will simply burn and fail to protect the beef. Nor should it be too thick. I usually ask for it one notch thicker than the deli would typically cut prosciutto.

Tying the string to secure the prosciutto can be tricky. There are numerous YouTube videos showing butcher's knots that make it look easy. However, as long as the prosciutto stays in place, that's what counts. Avoid lifting the beef roll by the string as you might accidentally cut through the prosciutto. Make sure to use butcher's twine or cotton string, as these are both food-safe and won't melt into your meat. My local supermarket stocks cotton string.

The beauty of this dish is that it can be cooked early on the day it's needed, then covered to rest and served just warm — making it perfect for transporting to the feast.

To make gravy from the pan juices, place the baking tin on the stove over low heat. Add two tablespoons of plain flour and mix it in to create a roux. Add a cup of red wine and stir, making sure to scrape up all the meat juices and crispy bits from the bottom of the tray.

- 1 kg girello beef
- 20 slices of prosciutto, not too thin
- 250 g Swiss brown mushrooms, sliced
- 1 clove of garlic, finely chopped
- 2 tbl butter
- Sea salt and black pepper, to taste
- Handful of fresh rosemary and thyme
- Squeeze of lemon juice

Preheat oven to 210°C fan/230°C with your roasting tray inside to warm up.

Pick leaves from the herbs. Spread herbs, salt and pepper on an oven tray, and roll beef to generously coat.

On a clean flat surface, lay a long piece of string horizontally and then 3-5 shorter pieces of string vertically, that will line up with the ends and middle of your piece of meat. Lay slices of prosciutto vertically along the string making sure that they overlap. Leave a couple of slices aside to help cover any gaps that appear when encasing the beef.

Gently melt butter in a frypan. Sauté mushrooms and garlic until soft. Add lemon juice. Gently spread mushrooms over the laid-out prosciutto. Place the beef in the middle of the prosciutto and fold the prosciutto over to fully encase it. You may need to use a couple of the extra slices. Tie the string to help secure the prosciutto in place.

Place the meat in the hot roasting tray and cook for 30 minutes. When cooked, take the meat out to rest for at least 5 minutes.

Return any juices to the pan and use to make a wonderful gravy to serve.

Slice as thickly as desired. Serve with crisp greens and roast potatoes.

https://youtu.be/4Evl2pHj4ew

Porchetta

Serves 6-8

Every culture has a dish reserved for special occasions. Porchetta is one of them—and today, we have two reasons to celebrate. Not only is this a festive Christmas roast to share with loved ones, but it also marks the 100th episode of Rie's Kitchen. Ten years ago, I never imagined we'd reach such a milestone!

In Italian, porchetta means pork, but this is no ordinary piece of pork. Using pork belly stuffed with minced pork and fresh herbs, the roll is slowly roasted to render fat and keep the meat tender and succulent. A final blast of high heat gives that perfect blistered crackling.

For crackling that's crispy all over, elevate the meat as it cooks—either on a rack or over sturdy vegetables like carrots. I usually add only water to the base of the tray to catch the drippings and keep moisture in. Some recipes use water and white wine, but I haven't found much difference. I'd rather enjoy a glass while it roasts.

Patience is key. The skin must be dry—so prep the night before. And don't rush the roast; slow cooking is crucial. The final challenge? Letting it rest before carving. Guard it from sneaky fingers eager to steal a crackling shard!

If you're lucky enough to have leftovers, they're brilliant in a ploughman's board or sandwich. I love thin slices with pickled cabbage.

True celebrations are slow and generous—just like this beautiful roast. Porchetta deserves to be the centrepiece.

- 150 g pork mince
- Sea salt
- Crushed peppercorns
- 2 cloves garlic, minced
- 1 tbl olive oil
- 1 slice stale bread, soaked in warm water
- 20 g grated Parmesan cheese
- 2 tbl chopped flat-leaf parsley

- 1 kg pork belly
- 6 sage leaves or 1 tbl fennel seeds, roasted and ground
- 2 sprigs rosemary
- 2 cloves garlic, minced
- Salt and pepper
- Bunch of parsley

- Olive oil
- Salt
- 500 ml water

Day before:

Score pork skin at 1–2cm intervals. Place pork belly on a baking rack over the sink and pour boiling water over the skin. Pat dry with paper towels. Scatter salt over the skin, rub into cuts, and transfer skin-side up to a baking paper–lined tray. Refrigerate uncovered overnight to dry out the skin.

To make stuffing:

Combine mince, salt, pepper, and garlic. Mix well with your hands, drizzle with olive oil and mix again. Squeeze liquid from bread and add to meat. Add 20g Parmesan and mix thoroughly. Add parsley and mix once more. Set aside.

Prep belly:

Place belly meat-side up and cut down the middle, then butterfly each half. Rub salt and pepper into the fat. Finely chop sage, rosemary, and garlic. Sprinkle herbs (include fennel if using) over the meat and rub in.

Spread stuffing over the centre of the belly and close the flaps. Sprinkle with more salt and pepper. Lay parsley (stalks and all) along one long edge. Roll away from you to enclose the parsley. Don't worry if there's a small gap.

Tie tightly with a 2m length of string.

Roasting:

Place a rack inside a large baking tray and set porchetta on top. Drizzle skin with olive oil, sprinkle with salt, and rub in. Add water to the bottom of the tray.

Preheat oven to 130°C fan/150°C.

Cook for 3 hrs, then increase to 230°C fan/250°C for 30 mins until the skin blisters.

Rest 30 mins before carving.

Gluten free pizza

Serves 4-6

Originally from Italy, the term 'pizza' was first documented in the 10th century. The modern pizza, as we know it today, was developed in Naples in the 18th century and has since become a global dish. In 2009, Neapolitan pizza was registered with the European Union as a Traditional Speciality Guaranteed dish.

Many cultures boast a similar dish - a bread base topped with simple ingredients and then baked or heated through.

There are numerous debates surrounding the perfect pizza - thick versus thin crust, tomato or BBQ sauce as a base, the divisive question of pineapple or not. However, this is such a simple dish to make at home that you can create them however you prefer. Personally, I like a thick crust, with a tomato-based sauce, lots of olives and anchovies, and definitely NO pineapple. Only your imagination limits you from becoming the master of your own pizzeria!

Creating gluten-free crispy crusts can be challenging. This simple recipe provides a thick crust that remains intact without absorbing the sauce. Using a pizza stone certainly assists in achieving that desirable crisp crust, but a metal oven tray will suffice too. If you're fortunate enough to have a pizza oven that utilises hot coals, the resulting flavour and texture will be amazing.

Dough:
- 2 cups self-raising flour (GF)
- 150 ml cream
- 150 ml milk

Topping:
- 5 tbl tomato sauce
- 100 g hot salami
- 1 red onion
- 75 g kalamata olives
- 200 g mozzarella cheese
- 6 button mushrooms
- 6 anchovy fillets

Preheat oven to 220°C fan/240°C, with pizza stone in the oven to heat up.

In a large bowl make a well in the flour. Add the cream. Add 100 ml of milk and using a flat blade knife, stir the mixture to form a dough. Add additional milk as required to ensure all the flour is taken up into the dough.

On a floured board, gently knead the dough until it forms a smooth ball. Roll out the dough to fit your pizza stone.

Lightly flour your pizza stone, then carefully place the dough on the stone. Bake for 10 minutes.

Whilst the base is cooking, prepare your toppings.

When the base is lightly golden, remove from the oven and add tomato sauce. Gently spread over the base and up to the edges. Then layer salami, onion, olives, anchovies, mushrooms and finally mozzarella cheese.

Return to the oven and bake for 15 minutes.

Pizza is cooked when the cheese is melted, and the base can easily be lifted from the stone and is golden underneath.

Allow to stand for a few minutes before slicing.

https://youtu.be/0qFAnQR6zBg

Home made fettuccine carbonara

Serves 2

This recipe is one of my absolute favourite comfort foods. It's just like giving yourself a big hug in a bowl!

Of course, you can serve carbonara sauce with spaghetti or tagliatelle, but for me, the silky ribbons of fettuccine provide the right ratio of pasta to sauce. Achieving that silky smoothness in your pasta is easy with the right equipment – a pasta machine. I've also used a rolling pin, and on one occasion, a full wine bottle (that's a story for another time :)). The pasta machine makes light work of the task and is also fun!

I've had my pasta machine since I was 15. I keep it in its original box and simply adore it. I've considered upgrading to an electric machine, but for just my family, the manual hand crank isn't burdensome to use and gives me lots of satisfaction. For those days when I just don't have the energy to make up the fettuccine, dried packaged pasta fills the need. It doesn't, however, possess the same level of love and care that a bowl of homemade pasta provides. Fresh pasta cooks much faster than dried, so be ready with your sauce before adding the pasta to the water.

If you're making pasta in a humid or warm room, the volume of liquid needed to achieve a soft pliable dough can vary. I sometimes find that I need to add an extra egg, especially if my eggs are a bit small. A large egg weighs 50-59g, an extra-large egg weighs 60-67g, and a jumbo one weighs 67-72g (including shell). If the dough is too dry, you can sprinkle on some water. If it's too sticky, add some extra flour. The perfect dough shouldn't stick to your fingers.

When cutting the pasta, it's important to keep the strands separated and floured. I use a pasta tree to do this, but I've also covered a broomstick with foil and hung it between two chairs to hang the pasta from.

Pasta:
- 200 g plain flour
- 2 extra-large eggs
- Pinch of salt

Carbonara sauce:
- 150 g bacon or pancetta, cut into fine batons (approx. 2 middle rashers)
- 15 g butter
- 1 egg + 1 egg yolk
- 1 clove garlic, peeled
- 20 g parmesan cheese, grated
- 50 ml cream
- Salt and pepper, to taste

Place the flour and salt in a mound on your bench. Make a well and break the eggs directly into the well.

Using a fork, slowly incorporate the flour into the eggs.

Continue to combine until a soft dough is formed. Knead gently until smooth. Wrap pasta dough in clingfilm and place in the fridge to rest for 30 minutes.

Using a pasta machine, roll into lengths approximately 25 cm long and 3-4 mm thick (This is usually using 3 or 4 adjustments on your pasta rollers).

Using the fettuccine cutter, or a sharp knife, cut into thin strips approx 5 mm wide.

Bring a large pot of salted water to the boil (¾ tsp salt per litre water).

Meanwhile melt butter in a large frypan, fry garlic for 2 minutes then remove from the pan. Add the bacon and fry for 5 minutes. Stir in the cream, bring to the boil and remove from the heat.

In a small bowl, beat the egg, yolk and parmesan.

Add pasta to the boiling water and cook for about 3 minutes. When cooked, drain the pasta - reserving about ½ cup of the pasta liquid. Return the pasta to the pot, add the bacon and cream mixture. Mix well. Add the egg mixture and mix well. If a little dry add a small amount of the reserved liquid.

Serve immediately, in individual bowls - sprinkle with chopped parsley and cracked pepper.

Ravioli

Serves 4-6

Growing up, food was more than just sustenance - it was all about family. And no other family favourite illustrated this better than Ravioli. We would all have our set tasks - dad made the pastry and the sauce, I made the filling, my brother brushed the rolled pasta with milk, and mum's job was the cooking.

It took all day and we would make around 40 dozen. Those not eaten on the day, would be frozen, uncooked, for another day. Freeze them on the trays first so that they don't get damaged. This reduces them breaking up when cooking at a later date. Any leftovers that had been cooked were deep-fried the next day for a snack, Yum!

Traditional Maltese ravioli pasta is made by rubbing lard into the flour and then adding water to make a dough. It has no eggs, and this produces a fairly heavy pasta, white in colour. When I was first diagnosed with Coeliac's disease I thought that converting my traditional recipes to gluten-free, was just a matter of substitution of GF plain flour for wheat-based plain flour. WRONG! In fact, my first attempt at GF ravioli turned into quite a disaster, with the traditional Maltese pasta dissolving into glue as the ravioli cooked. A very disappointed Rie that day!

So after many tries to perfect GF fresh pasta, here is my recipe for GF pasta. It is perfect for lasagne or fettuccine. My favourite though, will always be ravioli, especially when using homemade ricotta cheese.

Pastry:
- 250 g plain flour (GF)
- 50 g potato flour
- 1 tbl oil
- 4 eggs

Filling:
- 300 g ricotta cheese
- 2 large eggs
- Salt and pepper to taste
- 2 bunches flat-leaf parsley, finely chopped
- Milk

Sauce:
- 400 g tin crushed tomatoes (or 3-4 tbl tomato paste)
- 1 onion, finely chopped
- 2 cloves garlic, crushed
- Fresh oregano, chopped

Combine flours in a bowl.

Tip flours onto a clean bench and make a well.

Add oil and first 2 eggs into the well. Using a fork, gradually incorporate the flours into the eggs to form a paste and then the dough. Knead together, adding additional eggs one at a time as necessary.

Knead until smooth.

Allow dough to rest in the fridge for at least half an hour.

Place ricotta into a large bowl and break up using a potato masher.

Add salt, pepper and parsley. Mix well.

Add 2 eggs, lightly beaten and mix well.

The masher should make a slurp sound when lifted from the ricotta. If it doesn't, add another egg and mix well.

Divide the pastry into 4 pieces. Keep those not being used under a damp towel so as not to dry out. Roll out pastry into long strip at least 8 cm wide and 3-4 mm thick.

Using a teaspoon, place heaped spoonfuls of filling in the bottom third of the pastry approximately 4 cm (width of two fingers) space in between.

Using a pastry brush, paint milk around each spoonful of filling.

Fold pastry over to enclose filling.

Using cupped hands press around each blob of filling to seal edges.

Using a glass, cut each ravioli out and place on a floured tray until ready to cook. Keep covered with a moist tea-towel so as not to dry out.

You can reuse scraps of pastry and re-roll.

Sauce:

Gently fry the onion and garlic until translucent.

Add tinned tomatoes and oregano, stir well and simmer for 10 minutes.

Place ravioli into a large pot of boiling salted water. Boil for 6-8 minutes until cooked (They will be floating in the water).

Serve with sauce and grated parmesan cheese.

https://youtu.be/VGbU50cwXlQ

Quinoa tabouli

Serves 8-10

With Spring heading quickly towards Summer, the days are getting longer, the temperature warmer, and more activities are happening outside. Tabouli is perfect for barbecues, picnics, and family meals. This recipe is loosely based on the traditional Middle Eastern recipe. By replacing the wheat with quinoa, it is also easily converted to gluten-free.

- ½ cup quinoa grain, cooked according to package instructions and chilled
- 1 punnet cherry tomatoes, diced
- 1 Lebanese cucumber, diced
- 6 spring onions, finely chopped
- 1.5 cups flat-leaf parsley, chopped
- ½ cup mint, chopped
- Juice of 1 lemon
- 1 clove garlic, crushed
- Salt and pepper, to taste
- 2 tbl olive oil

In a large bowl, toss together tomatoes, cucumber, onions and herbs.

Stir in quinoa.

In a separate bowl, combine oil, garlic, salt, pepper and lemon juice. Whisk well.

Add dressing to the salad and toss well.

The flavours improve overnight.

https://youtu.be/P-IodP8ES1U

Great Southern Land

Australia is home. It's where my pantry always has a stash of lemon myrtle, Vegemite, and a few Tim Tams for good measure. But more than that, it's where I've cooked for friends on balconies, shared scones with neighbours, and learned the fine art of a good pavlova from my mum.

This chapter is a celebration of that. The simple pleasures of weekend baking, the joy of packing a few slices into a tin for a road trip, or laying out a full spread for a Sunday lunch — it's all part of what makes Aussie food culture so comforting. It's humble, honest, and always best when shared.

You'll find plenty of sweet things in here — friands, slices, a good old sponge with passionfruit icing, and my take on lemon delicious pudding. There's also a nod to our British roots with the crumble and pudding, and of course, the ever-controversial ANZAC biscuit (chewy or crunchy? I'm team chewy, for what it's worth).

On the savoury side, there are crowd-pleasers like sausage rolls, chicken parma, and zucchini slice — all of which can be made gluten-free without losing their soul. And then there's the crumbed mussels, a recipe that reminds me of summer holidays down the coast and coming home with sandy feet and a bucket of fresh shellfish.

Whether you're whipping up a frittata for brunch, baking a loaf of gluten-free sourdough, or indulging in a bit of nostalgia with jelly slice, these are recipes that speak to a particular kind of Australian experience — grounded, generous, and just a little bit sun-kissed.

This is the food I grew up with, the food I share, and the food I still crave when I've been away too long.

Freshly barbecued lunch by the sea at Neds Beach, Lord Howe Island

Gluten free ANZAC biscuits

Makes 12

History is often written by the victorious—predominantly men. The voices of women, minorities, and others are frequently missing from official narratives, or at best given fleeting recognition.

ANZAC Day, held on the 25th of April, commemorates the landing of Australian and New Zealand troops at Gallipoli in 1915 during the Great War. In both countries, this public holiday honours all servicemen and women who have served in war and peacekeeping operations. The day begins with a solemn dawn service, followed by parades of returned servicemen and women, and community celebrations filled with pride. The Gallipoli landing is often referred to as "the birth of our nation"—a decidedly masculine view of birth—but the sacrifice made by so many is one for which I am eternally grateful.

The story of the ANZAC biscuit showcases the resilience of women. These women bid farewell to troop ships bound for the other side of the world. It was a time of slow communication—by telegram or mail transported by ship. Telephones were far from common in homes, let alone in pockets, and telegrams were often dreaded, as they frequently brought bad news.

Edmonds, a classic New Zealand cookbook first published in 1908, is similar in spirit to the Australian Women's Weekly or CWA cookbooks. In my copy, gifted by my lovely Kiwi friend, Cara, there's a brief history of these biscuits, originally known as "Soldiers' Biscuits." Concerned about the nutritional value of the food supplied to their men, wives, mothers and girlfriends sought solutions. Any food sent had to survive the non-refrigerated ships of the Merchant Navy and remain edible for two months. These inventive women adapted a Scottish oats biscuit recipe. Adding to the challenge, most poultry farmers had enlisted, and eggs were scarce. Consequently, golden syrup or treacle was used as the binding agent.

By WWII, refrigeration had improved, and women could send other treats, like fruit cake, to the men away fighting. My grandfather, Arthur Thyne, served in the 2/24th Australian Infantry Battalion, which saw extensive service at Tobruk, Libya, manning the Red Line and participating in intense fighting in the Salient.

In this recipe, bicarbonate of soda is used to lend some lightness. When combined with an acid such as lemon juice or yoghurt, it releases carbon dioxide, creating a rapid reaction perfect for pancakes or muffins. Here, the bicarb reacts to temperatures above 80°C and releases carbon dioxide, forming a foaming mixture added to the dry ingredients. Only half the carbon dioxide is released in this reaction, which can cause a slightly soapy taste but also contributes to the golden yellow colour. That's why we use only a small amount in this recipe.

Regrettably, oats are not gluten-free according to Coeliac Australia. Thankfully, quinoa flakes offer a similar texture and a delightful nutty taste. Per 100g, quinoa and oats have similar kilojoule and protein content, with quinoa containing less fat, oats fewer carbohydrates and over four times more fibre.

The ANZAC biscuit tradition lives on. These biscuits remain a family favourite. The CWA continues to make and sell them, celebrating the bravery of men and the ingenuity of women.

- 120 g butter
- 2 tbl golden syrup
- ½ tsp bicarbonate of soda
- 2 tbl boiling water
- 80 g quinoa flakes
- 100 g caster sugar
- 150 g plain flour (GF)
- 60 g shredded coconut

Preheat oven to 130°C fan/150°C

Combine butter and golden syrup in a small saucepan. Stir over low heat until butter is melted.

In a separate bowl, combine bicarbonate soda and boiling water. Stir into butter mixture.

Combine all dry ingredients in a large bowl. Add butter mixture and mix well.

Drop rounded teaspoons of mixture about 4 cm apart on lined oven trays, and lightly press.

Bake in the middle of the oven, for 20 minutes or until slightly brown.

Cool on trays.

https://youtu.be/bV3GhWSqYvw

Apple and rhubarb crumble

Serves 4

Whenever I ask Myles if he wants dessert, his answer is always crumble or pie. He doesn't mind what the filling is, but crumble is definitely his favourite. Traditionally, crumble topping includes oats, but as oats are not gluten-free, other options are needed. Often, I swap oats for quinoa flakes, and you certainly could add quinoa to this recipe if you wanted to – I've used slivered almonds to add the texture and nutty flavour instead.

Rhubarb is an undervalued vegetable. In traditional Australian backyards, it is a staple plant, and my rhubarb crowns are in peak season at the moment. Rhubarb can be a little stringy. There are both red and green varieties – mine is red. Both work well in this recipe. Rhubarb leaves are poisonous to eat but are great in the compost.

Other variations to this recipe include apple and berries, stewed peaches or nectarines – whatever is in season. In this recipe, I have chosen to use muscovado sugar. You can, of course, replace this with brown sugar. Brown sugar is refined white sugar with molasses added back to it. Muscovado sugar is less refined, so it retains much of its molasses component. The amount of molasses determines whether it is "light" or "dark": the darker the sugar, the more molasses it contains. The major difference between the two sugars is taste, and it's especially noticeable in recipes where the sugar is a star ingredient.

Perfectly served with custard or ice cream – this dessert will become a family favourite.

- 1 kg Granny Smith apples
- 5 sticks of rhubarb
- 1 tsp orange zest
- 1 tbl muscovado sugar

Crumble:
- 150 g almond meal
- 1 tsp ground cinnamon
- 75 g muscovado sugar
- 30 g rice flour
- 30 g potato starch
- 60 g unsalted butter, diced
- 40 g slivered almonds

Peel, core and roughly chop apples. Chop rhubarb into 2 cm pieces.

Place apple, orange zest, sugar in a medium-sized pot with 50 ml water and gently cook until apples are soft. Add rhubarb and cook a further 5 minutes until rhubarb is beginning to soften.

Preheat oven to 160°C fan/180°C.

Place all crumble ingredients except almonds in a food processor and pulse until it resembles breadcrumbs.

Gently toast almonds.

Reserve 2 tablespoons of almonds and stir the remainder into crumble mixture.

Place fruit in a buttered 4-cup dish (or 4 individual dishes).

Cover with crumble, sprinkle reserved almonds on top and bake for 25 minutes until golden.

Allow to sit for 5 minutes before serving with vanilla ice cream or custard :)

https://youtu.be/PhB8S5Le5fE

Apple and rhubarb tart

Serves 6

Who doesn't love pie?

For those of us avoiding gluten, the thought of pie can be very depressing. Many commercially prepared pastries are bland, soggy and heavy. But don't despair.

I have developed a fabulous sweet shortcrust pastry that is perfect for pies and tarts. And teamed with my homegrown rhubarb, it's an absolute winner!

The skill to getting the perfect tart base is to "blind bake". This simply means lining the raw shell with baking paper and weighing it down with either ceramic baking beads or raw dried beans/rice. After baking the pie shell for 15 minutes, remove the beads and baking paper. Finish baking the pie shell for another 5 minutes. Allow the pie shell to cool before putting in the filling. The dried beans or raw rice can be stored and used again (but will be no good to cook and eat).

For this tart, I have used Stephanie Alexander's Burnt butter filling - it is delicious and converts well to gluten-free.

Sweet shortcrust pastry:
- 1½ cups cornflour
- ¼ cup soy flour
- ¼ cup custard powder (GF)
- 1 tbl caster sugar
- 125 g cold, chopped butter
- 1 egg white
- 4-5 tbl iced water

Filling:
- 3 apples, sliced
- 5 sticks rhubarb sliced finely
- 2 eggs
- ½ cup sugar
- 1 heaped tbl plain flour (GF)
- 125 g butter

Pastry:

Mix together dry ingredients. Using your fingertips, rub in the butter until the mixture resembles breadcrumbs.

Make a well in the middle and add the slightly beaten egg white and iced water 1 tbl at a time, until the pastry comes together.

Roll the pastry into a ball.

Roll out the pastry between 2 sheets of baking paper until it fits your tin(s).

Carefully line your tin(s). Using a sharp knife, trim off any excess.

Refrigerate for 20 minutes.

Preheat oven to 190°C fan/210°C.

Cover bottom of pastry with baking paper, and fill with baking beads.

Bake for 15 minutes.

Remove beads and baking paper.

Bake a further 5 minutes.

Allow pastry to cool before adding filling.

Filling:

Preheat oven to 190°C fan/210°C.

Arrange fruit in cooled pie case.

Beat eggs and sugar until thick and creamy. Add flour.

In a small saucepan melt butter until a deep golden colour.

Add butter to egg mixture.

Gently spoon mixture over the fruit.

Bake 15 minutes or until filling is set.

Delicious served warm or cold with cream.

https://youtu.be/OlVbBltvbRU

Jelly slice

Serves 12-15

Every year when I am volunteering at the Royal Melbourne Show, I just have to smile when I see the excited children's faces over the jelly slice on their tray. I too love jelly slice.

My mum wasn't a big fan, so we only ate jelly slice at other kids' parties. Despite our constant nagging, she never surprised us with jelly slice in our lunchbox.

My love for the crunch of the base, the creaminess of the middle and the wobble of the jelly hasn't abated.

By just using gluten-free tea biscuits, this recipe is easily converted to gluten-free, and no one can tell! So for all those kids out there, here is my version of Jelly Slice. To make this a Christmas version, do a second layer of green jelly on the top. From above, it still looks red, but when cut, it has a stained glass window effect.

Base:
- 250 g tea biscuits, crushed
- 185 g butter, melted

Middle:
- 400 g tin sweetened condensed milk
- 2 tsp gelatin
- Juice of 2 lemons
- ½ cup boiling water

Top:
- 1 packet red jelly crystals (85 g)
- 2 tsp gelatin
- 250 ml boiling water
- 200 ml cold water

Top:
Mix gelatine and jelly crystals together. Add to boiling water and stir until dissolved. Add cold water. Stir. Set aside to cool but not set.

Base:
Mix crushed biscuits and melted butter until well combined. Press into the base of a 25 cm x 30 cm slice tray that is lined with baking paper. Make sure it is pressed well into the corners. Refrigerate for 10 minutes.

Middle:
Dissolve gelatine in boiling water. Add lemon juice. Combine with condensed milk. Spread over the biscuit base. Refrigerate for 10 minutes.

Gently ladle jelly over slice. Chill for at least 90 minutes. Cut into squares to serve.

https://youtu.be/GDascitQ_Z4

Gluten free kingston biscuits

Makes 24

When I was a kid, I can honestly say I had never heard of Kingston biscuits. We seldom had "bought biscuits", and if we did, they were the classic assortment – never any of the "fancy" cream biscuits. By the mid-1980s, when I was in high school, we occasionally had the cream assortment for special occasions. Although Kingstons had been manufactured in Australia since 1926, they didn't become a standard biscuit in the cream assortment until 1984 – and what a revelation that was. An oaty, coconutty twin biscuit joined together with a milk chocolate cream.

Now, as a coeliac, most commercial biscuits are off limits due to the use of oats, wheat flour, and many of the thickeners also used. As a proud member of the Country Women's Association of Victoria, I often bake for cake stalls and "pop-up" shops. One of the CWA mainstay biscuits is Yo-yos. I find these far too sweet for my tastes, so to have a gluten-free cream biscuit option, I began to work on a recipe for Kingstons as an alternative. I can honestly say that my Kingstons sell well to those seeking a gluten-free alternative, as well as to those on regular diets. It's probably the chocolate!

Why isn't chocolate always gluten-free? There are two explanations for why gluten finds its way into chocolate products. It's either included in an ingredient added to flavour the chocolate, such as in a cookies and cream chocolate bar. Alternatively, it's used as a thickener.

"If you use a very good chocolate then there is no gluten in it," says confectioner Jodie Neilson from New Farm Confectionery in Brisbane. "If you choose a very good, high percentage dark chocolate, then there also shouldn't be any milk solids in it either." (https://agfl.com.au/is-chocolate-gluten-free/)

Therefore, it's important that you always read the label on any chocolate you buy. High-percentage dark chocolate is always a good starting point. To make these, I use at least 70% cacao chocolate. I find up to 85% cacao is also delicious, but any higher and the ganache's bitterness isn't balanced by the biscuit's sweetness.

- 160 g salted butter, at room temperature
- 115 g brown sugar
- 1 tbl golden syrup
- 1 extra-large egg
- 200 g plain flour (GF)
- 80 g shredded coconut
- 50 g quinoa flakes

Filling:
- 200 g dark chocolate
- 30 g unsalted butter

Preheat oven to 180°C fan/200°C.

Line 2 large baking trays with baking paper.

Cream together butter and brown sugar until light in colour.

Add in egg and golden syrup and beat again until fluffy.

Fold in flour, coconut and quinoa flakes until it comes together into a smooth dough.

Take a small teaspoon of dough and round into balls (approximately 8 g each). Place onto prepared trays a few centimetres apart and press down with your fingers. They will spread a little.

Bake for 6-8 minutes until golden brown. Cool on the tray.

Filling:

Place chocolate and butter in a microwave-safe bowl. Microwave on high for 30 seconds. Stir well and microwave for another 30 seconds. Mix well and the last of the chocolate will melt and the mixture will thicken and resemble ganache.

Working quickly, take a teaspoon of the chocolate mix and place a dollop onto the flat side of one biscuit. Pop another biscuit on top and press down together. Allow to set for 5 minutes before enjoying with a cuppa!

https://youtu.be/vKCVXKBAY2o

Lemon delicious pudding

Serves 6

When I was in Year 7 in 1978, all students had to take a subject called Home Economics. The boys took it for one term and then moved on to woodwork and metalwork, while the girls stayed in "home ec." It was a different era—no one seemed concerned about this gender-specific curriculum. Although I was keen to try metalwork, I didn't mind staying in Home Economics. We learnt to cook some tasty dishes that still influence my cooking today. Our textbook, "Cookery the Australian Way," first published in 1966, has become an Australian classic. Written by Life Members of Home Economics Victoria (https://www.homeeconomics.com.au/curriculum-support/cookery-the-australian-way), I still find its explanations valuable for both recipes and the science behind the cooking. My copy is showing its age, but it's clearly well-loved.

"Lemon Delicious" was one of the first recipes we all learnt. The magic of watching a batter turn into a cake on top with a rich sauce below taught us various cooking techniques—like creaming butter and sugar, separating eggs, whipping egg whites, folding, and using a bain-marie. A bain-marie is a water bath used to gently heat food or keep it warm. In this case, we use it to gently heat our ramekins so the cake cooks while the sauce remains liquid. This was one of my earliest experiences of making something from scratch that usually came in a packet. I remember cooking "Lemon Delicious" for my grandmother, who was not one to give praise lightly. Her verdict: "You can cook this again." I took that as high praise.

My take on this classic dish diverges slightly from the one in my old textbook. After looking through CWA cookbooks, PWMU cookbooks, and recipes by Australian icon chefs like Stephanie Alexander and Maggie Beer, I found variations in ingredient quantities and the sequence of adding them. However, all versions yield a light, fluffy cake and a luscious citrus sauce. It's also an easy conversion from gluten-free flour to wheat flour with no changes needed in amounts or rising agents. This is a recipe you're likely to have all the ingredients for, and it's sure to please the whole family.

I prefer making six individual servings, but you can also use a 6-cup dish and bake at 160°C (fan-forced) for 1 hour, or until the cake is golden and springs back to the touch.

- 60 g salted butter, at room temperature
- 330 g caster sugar
- Zest of 1 lemon (approx. 1 tsp)
- 125 ml lemon juice (approx. 2 lemons)
- 3 large eggs, separated
- 375 ml milk
- 3 tbl self-raising flour (GF) (30 g)
- Extra butter for greasing
- Cream, to serve

Preheat oven to 160°C fan/180°C.

Grease six 1 cup ovenproof dishes/ramekins with butter.

In a large bowl, cream butter, caster sugar and lemon zest until pale. Add egg yolks and mix well.

Add ⅓ flour and mix well. Then add ⅓ milk and mix. Continue alternating flour and milk mixing well in between to form a smooth batter.

Add lemon juice and stir.

In a separate bowl, whip egg whites until stiff.

Gently fold egg whites into batter.

Ladle the batter into the ramekins. Place ramekins in a baking dish. Pour hot water into baking dish, to come halfway up sides of ramekins.

Bake for 45 minutes.

Allow to cool a little before serving with a dusting of icing sugar and cream.

https://youtu.be/DPKn5aq-czk

Gluten free lemon and poppyseed muffins

Makes 12

Classic combinations are hard to beat, and lemon with poppy seeds is definitely one of these. The combination is found in many cuisines, and a quick search on the internet for lemon and poppy seed muffins brings up hundreds of results – I am very grateful that you are looking at mine :)

Poppy seeds are an ancient Sumerian spice first cultivated in Mesopotamia around 3400 BC. When Alexander the Great conquered Egypt, this marked the beginning of spices, including poppy seeds from the Middle East, being imported into Greece. This was also when the use of poppy seeds in bread began. The use of poppy seeds in Europe continued through the Middle Ages, serving as both medicine and spice. Today, the world's main poppy seed producer is the Czech Republic, followed by Turkey and Spain. They add a lovely subtle nutty flavour and a bit of crunch to this recipe.

Many lemon and poppy seed recipes use sour cream, but I prefer Greek yoghurt. Whole milk Greek yoghurt and sour cream can be directly substituted 1:1. The yoghurt adds a tangy texture that I believe complements the lemon juice and zest, enhancing the citrus flavour. Avoid using low-fat yoghurt – the thickeners and stabilisers used in low-fat yoghurt can impart a chalky flavour to your finished baked product.

In this recipe, I use almond flour. It adds a fine texture to the crumb of the muffins and provides some stability that gluten-free plain flour doesn't have. Replacing almond flour with more plain flour will give you a more cake-like consistency. Almond flour is different to almond meal. Almond flour is made from blanched, peeled almonds, while almond meal is made from raw, unpeeled almonds. Almond meal is coarser, with brown flecks from the skin, and can be slightly bitter.

The muffin batter is quite thick. For best results in achieving a lovely domed top, use an ice cream scoop. This also ensures evenly sized muffins. Not all ice cream scoops are the same size. It is important to know the volume of your tins. I have two muffin tins with quite different sized cups. In my older tin, I use a Size 12 (70 ml) ice cream scoop, and in my modern tin, I use a Size 20 (45 ml). This also affects the patty tin liners you buy. The liners at the supermarket don't always have size or capacity listed on the packets. For the most professional results, a baking supplier will have a range of clearly sized liners in a wide array of colours and patterns.

- 280 g plain flour (GF)
- 80 g almond flour
- 150 g caster sugar
- 2 tsp baking powder
- 1 tsp baking soda
- 1 tsp xanthan gum
- ½ tsp salt
- Zest of 3 lemons
- 2 tbl poppy seeds
- 130 g unsalted butter, at room temperature
- 140 g Greek/natural yoghurt
- 2 large eggs
- 4 tbl lemon juice

Icing piped in stripes:
- 200 g soft icing mix
- 1 tbl lemon juice
- 2 tbl milk

Preheat oven 190°C fan/210°C.

Line a 12 hole muffin tin with paper liners.

In a large bowl whisk together flours, caster sugar, baking powder, baking soda, xanthan gum, salt, lemon zest and poppy seeds.

Add the butter and using a mixer, beat until resembling breadcrumbs.

In a separate bowl whisk together the eggs, lemon juice and yoghurt.

Add egg mixture to the flours and beat until you have a thick smooth batter with no lumps of flour.

Using an ice-cream scoop, divide the mixture into the liners. The batter is quite thick and will keep the shape of the scoop.

Bake 18-20 minutes until risen, golden brown and a skewer comes out clean.

Allow to cool in the tin for 5 minutes before placing on a cake rack to cool.

When cold ice.

Store in an airtight container.

Icing

Mix together the ingredients to make a paste of piping consistency. Using a piping bag with a fine nozzle (size 6) pipe zigzags across each muffin.

https://youtu.be/GtJnK3fwK9w

Gluten free lime and coconut friands

Makes 12

Lime and coconut friands are a favourite in our house. Limes are plentiful for 10 months of the year from our tree, and being gluten-free they are a treat we can both share. So, they were a logical pick to be the first ever video on our YouTube Channel in 2014. I'm a bit nervous in the video, my apron doesn't even have a logo on it, and I soon learned that more clear glass bowls were needed. Myles would probably want to re-edit this if he had a chance too - we have become much "slicker" in our camera shots, straight to camera advice, and editing.

No matter what changes we would make to the video, there is no need to change this recipe - moist cakes with the crunch of toasted coconut. What's not to love!

- 6 egg whites
- 40 g soy flour
- 40 g shredded coconut
- 90 g LSA meal
- 240 g pure icing sugar
- 2 tbl lime juice
- 2 tsp fine lime zest
- 185 g butter, melted
- 10 g additional shredded coconut

Preheat oven to 180°C fan/200°C.

Grease 12-hole friand pan (½ cup).

Whisk egg whites, using a fork, in a bowl until well combined and frothy. Add meal, sifted sugar and flour, butter, zest, juice, and coconut. Stir until combined.

Divide mixture evenly among pan holes.

Bake friands in the middle of the oven for 10 minutes.

Remove from oven and sprinkle each friand with additional coconut.

Bake a further 10 minutes.

Stand in the pan for 5-10 minutes. Remove from pan and place on a wire rack to cool.

Friands can be stored in an airtight container for 3 days or frozen for up to 1 month.

Pavlova

Serves 6-8

No Aussie family function, picnic, BBQ, birthday, or "bring a plate" event is complete without some version of the Pavlova or "pav". I know my New Zealand friends will argue that the pavlova was a Kiwi invention. But, where it was developed is really irrelevant, it is one of those Aussie/Kiwi national dishes that helps define us.

The base of the pavlova is made from meringue. Bought bases tend to be crisp and quite hollow. Homemade bases tend to have more of the soft gooey marshmallow-like middle. The meringue is made from beaten egg whites.

Important tips:

- The bowl must be very clean, free from all grease, otherwise, the egg whites won't beat to a stiff peak.
- Eggs need to be at room temperature to get maximum volume.
- Dress with cream, etc at the last possible moment to keep the base crisp.

Common problems:

- Oozing liquid from the meringue - it is undercooked.
- Syrupy droplets forming on the outside of the meringue shell - it is overcooked.

Now over the years, my family got into a set routine for the toppings on the pav. Strawberries and passion fruit or crushed peppermint crisp. Myles's family often used kiwi fruit. My aunt used drained crushed pineapple. In France 2014, I made one using bananas and wild strawberries. What you decorate it with is up to you, and what you have on hand.

- 4 egg whites, at room temperature
- Pinch of salt
- 2 tsp white wine vinegar
- 2 tsp cornflour
- 1 tsp gluten-free vanilla extract
- 250 g caster sugar
- 1 tsp cinnamon (optional)

Vanilla whipped cream:

- 600 ml cream
- ½ tsp gluten-free vanilla extract
- ½ vanilla pod, seeds scraped (optional)

Traditional toppings:

- 1 punnet of strawberries, sliced
- 1 kiwi fruit, sliced
- 1 passion fruit, pulp
- 1 peppermint crisp, crushed

Preheat oven to 100°C fan/120°C with the rack in the bottom ⅓ of the oven.

Use individual sized ramekins to trace circles with a pencil onto greaseproof paper. Line a baking sheet with the greaseproof paper, marking side up.

In a small bowl, mix the cinnamon and sugar together. Keep aside. In the bowl of an electric mixer, fitted with the whisk attachment, beat egg whites on low-speed until they are frothy. Add the salt, vinegar, and corn flour and beat on medium speed until soft peaks form. This will take between 3-4 minutes. Add the sugar mixture in 3 additions, mixing well between each addition. Beat on medium-high speed until meringue is stiff and glossy, between 3-5 minutes. Add vanilla extract and seeds if using and mix until combined.

Divide the meringue evenly between the marked circles on the greaseproof paper and use the back of a spoon to thin out the centre of the Pavlova, creating a well, while building up the sides as you fill in the circles. You want the outer walls of the Pavlova to be at least 3cm high. Bake until the meringue is glossy and hard to the touch, about 1 hour and 30 minutes.

* Normally a Pavlova is bright white and you would reduce the temperature if it began to take on too much colour. Due to the addition of the cinnamon these Pavlova will be slightly golden in colour anyway.

When the Pavlova is cooked through, turn off the oven and leave the Pavlova to cool in the oven for at least 2-3 hours or overnight. When completely cooled the Pavlova will lift easily from the greaseproof paper. Keep in an airtight container for up to 2 days.

Vanilla Whipped Cream:

Whip cream and vanilla together until thick.

Plating:

Spoon the whipped cream onto the shell, then let your artistic streak shine as you decorate with the fruit and chocolate.

https://youtu.be/LbmoMzin1wc

Raspberry coconut slice

Serves 12

Sometimes you just can't beat a classic recipe, and this is one of them. A very "retro classic", Raspberry and Coconut slice was made popular in the post-war period. Here in Australia, it appeared in the Australian Women's Weekly and The Country Women's Association Cookbooks in the 1950s, but I suspect that the recipe is much older than that. My version is very similar to these, and apart from using gluten-free flours, I am much more generous with the jam.

This recipe is also a rare one, in that it allows a direct swap for "normal flour" to be replaced with commercially available gluten-free flour. As the base is a biscuit-like consistency, there is no need to add extra rising agents, or strong flours like tapioca or potato. It just works! Myles took the slice to work and didn't tell anyone that it was Gluten-Free - no one could tell - and it was all devoured. The most important ingredient is the raspberry jam - don't skimp on the jam and use the best quality you can. Obviously, as a jam maker, I use my own raspberry jam, which is less sweet than many commercially available jams. This recipe would also be delicious with blackberry jam, lemon curd, etc. - the possibilities are only limited by your pantry!

Base:
- 90 g butter, at room temperature
- 110 g caster sugar
- 1 egg
- 50 g self-raising flour (GF)
- 100 g plain flour (GF)
- 250 ml raspberry jam

Topping:
- 2 eggs, lightly beaten
- 75 g caster sugar
- 180 g shredded coconut

Preheat oven to 160°C fan/180°C.
Grease a 20 cm x 30 cm slice pan.

Cream butter and sugar with an electric mixer. Add egg and mix well.
Stir in flours.
Spread the mixture evenly over the base of the prepared slice pan.
Bake for 12 minutes.

Combine all topping ingredients together and mix well.

When the base is ready, remove from oven. Whilst it is still hot, spread jam evenly.
Carefully spread topping over jam.
Return to oven and bake for a further 30 minutes.

Allow to cool in the tin. When cool, run a palette knife around the edges, as sometimes the jam can stick a little bit. Turn out onto a rack, and cut into twelve portions.

Perfect served with a cuppa. It will keep for 2-3 days in an airtight container.

https://youtu.be/ODjhYhd14Aw

Raspberry pistachio friands

Makes 12

These friands are so easy to make. They are unbelievably good warm "just out of the oven" with a cuppa.

As a jam maker, I always have raspberries in the freezer. A few years ago, my good friend Val Smith found some friand recipes in a magazine. She remembered me explaining to her that friands are often gluten-free, or at least easy to convert. So Val gave me a set of friand recipes. I have to admit that having modified this one to be gluten-free, and it being so good, I haven't ever tried any of the others. This one is just too hard to pass up!

As with ALL gluten-free baking, it is essential that you allow the cooked friands to cool in the tray until the tray can be handled with your bare hands. Then, and only then, do you remove them and place them on a wire rack to cool completely. This gives the friand ingredients time to solidify, and in this case, enables you to get them out of the tray in one piece.

A friand is a small French cake, often mistaken for a muffin. The principal ingredients are usually almond meal, egg whites, butter, and sugar. Typically, they are baked in small oval moulds or tins. If you don't have a friand tray, they work well as muffins too - use a ½ cup muffin tin. And of course, you could use "ordinary" wheat-based plain flour too.

- ¾ cup almond meal
- ¼ cup finely ground pistachios
- 1⅔ cup icing sugar, sifted
- ¾ cup GF plain flour
- ¾ tsp xanthan gum
- ¼ tsp GF baking powder
- 5 egg whites
- 125 g butter, melted
- 200 g raspberries (fresh or frozen - no need to defrost)
- 2 tbl pistachios, finely chopped (extra)

Preheat oven to 180°C fan/200°C.

Place the almond meal, ground pistachios, icing sugar, flour, xanthan gum, baking powder, egg whites and butter into a bowl. Whisk until just combined. Fold through the raspberries.

Spoon into a 12 x ½ cup lightly greased friand tray or muffin tin.

Sprinkle with the chopped pistachios and bake for 20-25 minutes or until golden and cooked through.

Allow to cool in the trays. Use a palette knife to gently remove the friands and place them onto a wire rack to cool completely.

Gluten free scones

Makes 12

Scones are a simple treat, steeped in tradition. They're easy to make at home, but more often savored at Devonshire Teas or as part of High Tea. Some people believe that the jam should be spread first, followed by the cream, while others vehemently argue for the reverse. An internet search reveals many variations on the basic recipe, some using lemonade or butter. Growing up, both my mum and grandmother used the recipe on the "Sunshine powdered milk" tin. Searching for gluten-free scones also yields surprising results, with many recipes incorporating mashed potato! Of course, there are also date scones, herb scones, pumpkin scones, and fruit scones.

When one thinks of the Country Women's Association (CWA), scones are usually in the picture. As a proud member of the CWA of Victoria, I've helped many great cooks serve our famous scones at various functions including the Royal Melbourne Show, High Teas, get-togethers, and Australia Day celebrations at Government House. The public constantly requests our recipe, with many finding it hard to believe how simple it is.

After numerous trials to perfect a light, fluffy gluten-free scone, I've settled on this "no-fail" recipe. The addition of tapioca flour (arrowroot) and cornflour lends lightness to the scones, regardless of the brand of self-raising flour used. This straightforward scone recipe is easy to whip up when unexpected guests drop by.

The techniques used here are a combination of tips learned from some of the great bakers at the CWA. Joy Davies, the chief scone cook at the Royal Melbourne Show, insists on only using a knife to mix the ingredients — not a spoon, and especially not a wooden spoon as it "sucks the air out of the dough". She also recommends patting out the dough rather than rolling it. Pam Mawson always uses an egg wash to achieve a great, even color on the scone tops. Noela McLeod insists on not twisting the scone cutter to keep the scones straight. Both Joy and Noela brush the baked scones with melted butter for that final touch.

- 3 cups self-raising flour (GF)
- 1 cup tapioca flour
- 4 tbl cornflour
- 1 tsp baking powder
- 300 ml cream
- 300 ml milk

- 1 egg
- Dash of milk

- Self raising flour for dusting

Preheat oven to 225°C fan/245°C.

Combine all dry ingredients in a large bowl. Make a well and add cream and milk. Using a cutting motion, mix together to form a soft dough.

Turn dough out onto a floured surface and lightly knead. Pat out the dough to a thickness of 2.5 cm. Using a floured scone cutter, cut out scones and place onto a baking tray lined with baking paper.

Lightly beat egg and a dash of milk in a separate bowl. Brush the tops of each scone with egg wash.

Bake for 12-15 minutes. The bottom of the scones should be a pale brown in colour.

Wrap in a tea-towel for a few minutes to steam.

Serve with jam and cream.

https://youtu.be/xKhqK_9ZbSc

Sponge cake with passionfruit icing

Serves 8

What family celebration or community event isn't better with a homemade passionfruit sponge?

At just about every CWA (Country Women's Association) event, the passionfruit sponge is a standout when everyone is asked to "bring a plate" to share. I had always thought these delightful cushions of air—served with whipped cream, jam or fresh strawberries, and topped with passionfruit icing—were difficult to make and best left to the masters. But that's not the case. With a few simple tips, you too can wow the crowd with this easy, delicious treat.

Being Coeliac, I use maize-based cornflour. Some of my CWA friends prefer wheat-based cornflour, as it gives a greater rise. This allows them to split each cake so the recipe makes two filled sponges.

Being a CWA member is an absolute joy. The ladies are always keen to share their collective wisdom.

1. At a Prahran Market event a few years ago, Noela McLeod, then National President of CWA of Australia, asked us to bring in failed sponges so she could discuss the issues with the crowd. My "rubber dunlops" were presented to Noela, who said, "You didn't have to try this hard," with a wink. "What did you do?" The solution was mixing too timidly—you really need to whip those eggs. Don't be afraid.
2. I also had the sponge stick to the sides of the tin. I'd used a commercial "spray" that was ineffective and also coloured the outside too much. My good friend Carol Clay, former State President of CWA Victoria, allowed me to share her secret—see note below.
3. For egg selection, Rosalyn Heaney recommends not using eggs that are too fresh—they won't whip well. Carol also suggests keeping eggs at room temperature and warming them in warm water in the mixing bowl while you prep your tins to add extra lightness.
4. My dear friend Val Smith shared these tips: Weigh your tins to ensure they're even. Put a slight dip in the batter's centre to level the top as it rises. Bang the tin on the bench before it goes in the oven to remove large air bubbles.
5. Finally, Pam Mawson, a CWA judge, recommends covering your wire rack with a tea towel before turning out the cake. This prevents grid marks.

Such a wonderful collection of tried and tested wisdom from these generous women!

- 4 eggs
- Pinch of salt
- ¾ cup caster sugar
- ¾ cup cornflour
- 1 tsp cream of tartar
- ½ tsp bicarbonate of soda
- 1 tsp vanilla extract

To decorate:
- 300 ml whipped cream
- Strawberries

Passionfruit Icing:
- 1-2 passionfruit
- 1 cup icing sugar

Preheat oven to 165°C fan/185°C.

Separate eggs. Beat egg whites with a pinch of salt until soft peaks form. Gradually beat in caster sugar until glossy and stiff peaks form.

Fold in egg yolks and vanilla. Fold in sifted dry ingredients until well combined.

Pour mixture into 2 x 20 cm (8") tins that have been well greased.

Bake in the middle of the oven for 20-25 minutes, or until the sides of the cake have shrunk a little away from the sides of the tin.

Carefully turn cakes out onto a wire rack that is covered with a tea-towel. Allow to cool before decorating.

Passionfruit icing:

Mix together sifted icing sugar and approximately 1 tablespoon of passionfruit pulp. Place bowl over hot water, stirring until it is the right consistency, then apply to cake.

Carol's secret tip for preparing your tins:

Melt approximately 1 tablespoon of Copha. Add sufficient flour (in this case cornflour to keep it gluten-free) and mix until it becomes a paste, about the consistency of icing. Brush thickly onto the sides of the tin. Any leftover mix can be stored in the fridge and warmed up for the next batch.

https://youtu.be/J_yfBdzhxXY

Dark chocolate rocky road

Serves 16

To quote a famous resident on Sesame Street, Rocky Road is definitely "sometimes food". That's what makes it perfect for Christmas celebrations and homemade gifts. The combinations of flavours are endless. What you're after is colour scattered generously throughout, where every bite has crunch, softness and sweetness.

My rocky road is definitely for grown-ups. I use only 70% couverture chocolate, preferring Plaistowe brand, fresh pomegranate Turkish delight that melts in your mouth, and the fabulous pop of green in the pistachios to give it crunch. Of course, you can use milk chocolate or a half-and-half mix. Melts are great, and if the kids are helping, they can make the job easier.

The addition of coconut oil may be new to some of you. The oil adds a nice shine, improves the mouthfeel of the chocolate, and makes it easier to cut into bite-sized chunks or bars. I use a pizza cutter to cut this up—easier to get nice straight lines if cutting into bars to give as gifts.

Just a note, not all marshmallows are gluten-free, especially the very small ones. It might save you some preparation time, but it will impact who you can share these with.

- 500 g dark chocolate (70%)
- 2 tbl coconut oil
- 290 g marshmallows, halved (about 3 cups tightly packed)
- 200 g fresh Turkish delight – I use pomegranate and rose
- 25 g shredded coconut (about ⅓ cup)
- 85 g shelled pistachios, chopped in half

Break the chocolate into small pieces. Place into a large heatproof bowl. Add the coconut oil. Melt over a pot of boiling water, stirring constantly and being careful that the bowl doesn't touch the water.

Add all the other ingredients and mix well.

Place into a 20 cm square tin lined with baking paper. Chill for 2–3 hours until set.

Remove from the fridge and allow to come to room temperature, about 30 minutes. This makes it easier to cut.

Keep refrigerated if living in a warm or humid climate.

https://youtu.be/8Uw9xyN01w4

Asparagus with speck and gorgonzola

Serves 4

Nothing says spring like fresh asparagus. As the delicate spears start to poke through the ground, they are as strong a symbol of the weather warming as the dancing daffodils in my flower beds.

This dish is perfect for a special occasion or to add some "wow" factor to a dinner party. It is simple to prepare and takes only minutes to put together. Don't be put off by the Gorgonzola. The creaminess and picante add so much depth to this dish without being overpowering.

This very special dish is my take on a side dish that I discovered in Taupo, New Zealand, a few years ago. We had spent the day kayaking across Lake Taupo and were quite hungry. In the main restaurant area of Taupo, we found a wine bar and food store that had some funky lighting and a bit of buzz. Initially, we were looking for a snack, but we ended up staying for dinner.

The menu mainly consisted of Tapas. To our great delight, this asparagus dish was amazing! Later in the evening, the chef popped out to speak with guests. I checked with him that I had decoded the ingredients correctly. I asked to have a photo taken with him. I have the biggest grin, and disturbingly, on reviewing the photo, he had most of his fingers covered with blue bandaids! They certainly weren't caused by this dish - no tricky techniques with this one.

- Olive oil
- 1 large red onion, chopped
- 100 g speck, diced
- 2 bunches of green asparagus
- Balsamic vinegar
- 100 g Gorgonzola, crumbled into small pieces

In a frypan, heat a little olive oil. Gently sweat the onions until they start to caramelise. Remove from the pan.

Add speck to the pan and toss on high heat until the speck is crispy.

Meanwhile, blanch the asparagus.

Return the onions to the frypan with the speck and warm through. De-glaze the pan with balsamic vinegar.

Arrange the asparagus on a serving dish. Pour over the onions and speck. Sprinkle with Gorgonzola.

Allow the cheese to melt and then serve.

https://youtu.be/NrQQfIIAo3Y

Aussie sausage rolls

Makes 12

To badly misquote Bon Scott, "It's a long way to the shop if you want a sausage roll."

In my childhood, there was rarely a birthday party or family gathering where sausage rolls did not appear. Up until my later primary school years, they were always homemade, but then more commercially-made options became available. Party sausage rolls are still available in the freezer section of supermarkets, in packs of 12 or 24. These 2-3 cm bite-sized treats remain popular for feeding multi-generational crowds, but nothing beats homemade ones.

In 2020, as Melbourne was learning the rhythm of life in lockdown, the Country Women's Association of Victoria began hosting fortnightly pop-up shops, initially as a fundraiser but more importantly as a community event. Our long, sweeping driveway allowed for drive-thru service with minimal contact. Freshly baked scones and a rotation of other baked goods were on offer. As the token coeliac, I always provided at least one gluten-free option. Then in April, Deputy State President Pam Mawson told me we were going to offer sausage rolls at the next pop-up—could I make some that were gluten-free? I had to admit I hadn't made any for well over 30 years, let alone gluten-free ones. But the challenge was set.

First, I joined the team working with Pam in the gargantuan effort of making 700 "ordinary" sausage rolls. With lots of laughter under masks and much chatting, it's amazing anything got baked that day, but secrets were shared.

I went home to make these gluten-free, and they were a big hit!

There is always a lot of discussion among CWA members regarding any recipe, and this one is no different—especially concerning the choice of meat. You can purchase a product called "sausage meat," sold in a tube and with a very gluggy texture from being minced very finely. The consensus among CWA cooks is that it has the wrong consistency and is also too fatty. Hence, in this recipe, I use beef and pork sausages and just remove the skins.

A special note for gluten-free fresh breadcrumbs: If you're using commercially produced sliced bread—the kind bought in plastic bags at the supermarket—you'll need to lightly toast the bread before putting it in your food processor. Otherwise, the bread will form a moist clump and be difficult to break up. I tend to save the crusts from my homemade sourdough loaves, which don't need to be toasted first.

There's no end to the variety of sausage roll fillings—try chicken mince, pork with apple and fennel, or pork with lemongrass, ginger, and chilli, just to name a few.

- 250 g beef mince
- 250 g pork mince
- ½ cup grated onion (1 medium onion)
- ½ cup grated carrot (1 medium carrot)
- 2 tsp crushed garlic
- 1 tsp salt
- 1 tbl mixed herbs
- 1½ cups fresh breadcrumbs
- 2 sheets puff pastry
- 1 egg
- ½ cup milk

Line a large baking tray with baking paper.

Into a large bowl place the mince, onion, carrot, garlic, salt, herbs, and breadcrumbs. Using your hands, mix well to combine. Divide the mixture into 4.

In a small bowl beat together the egg and milk.

Working with one pastry sheet at a time, cut in half horizontally. Take ¼ of the mixture and form it into a log along the middle of the pastry rectangle. Using a pastry brush, brush some egg wash along the long edge of the pastry. Fold the pastry over and press over the join. Use a fork to crimp the edges.

Cut the roll into 3 (approx 5 cm) and place on the tray.

Repeat with remaining ingredients.

Brush all sausage rolls with the egg wash and using a sharp knife make 3 slashes along the top to release steam and ensure your pastry remains crisp.

Bake for 20 minutes until golden.

Serve with tomato sauce or chutney.

https://youtu.be/PXSXdIRYZoQ

Chicken and mushroom pie

Serves 4

Classic food combinations become classics because they've stood the test of time. Chicken paired with leek and mushrooms is one such timeless blend, as is the interplay between flaky pastry and creamy sauce. This pie is certainly greater than the sum of its parts! Mastering the simple techniques in a chicken and mushroom pie allows you to adapt the dish to your family's preferences and tastes.

Pie making is definitely a skill worth learning. Using gluten-free pastry, as I do, adds an extra layer of complexity, but it's not insurmountable. For this recipe, I've used commercial puff pastry, but you can certainly make your own. The resulting butteriness perfectly complements this pie.

The type of pie dish determines whether you need a pastry bottom as well as a top. A casserole dish only requires a "hat", whereas a solid pie dish gives you the option. If you use a perforated pie dish, like I do, then a pastry base and lid are essential. Gluten-free pastry can be quite soggy, and the perforated dish ensures a crisp base without the need for blind baking.

Blind baking is a technique used to pre-bake the base of the pie, ensuring crispness. Wikipedia defines it as the process of baking a pie crust or other pastry without the filling. It's necessary when the filling will not be baked or has a shorter baking time than the crust.

In my Chicken and Mushroom Pie, I create a roux by adding flour to the pan with the butter, leeks, and chicken and cooking it briefly before adding the stock. This thickens the sauce, ensuring the filling doesn't ooze out during cooking or when cut to serve. If you prefer a less thick sauce, you can adjust the amount of flour, but you'll need to use a pie bird to vent the steam, preventing the filling from bubbling over and a soggy crust. A pie bird is a hollow ceramic tool, often shaped like a bird.

I usually serve this pie with baked potatoes and crisp green beans.

- 200 g Swiss brown button mushrooms, quartered
- 3 chicken thighs, cut into bite-sized pieces
- 1 tbl olive oil
- 2 tbl butter
- 1 leek, finely chopped
- 40 g plain flour
- 175 ml chicken stock
- 1 tsp Dijon mustard
- 3 tbl crème fraîche
- A couple of sprigs of rosemary and thyme
- ½ tsp ground nutmeg
- 2 sheets puff pastry
- 1 egg
- Splash of milk
- Salt and pepper

Preheat oven to 170°C fan/190°C.

In a large frypan heat olive oil and butter. Add leek and gently sauté until soft. Add chicken and gently brown. Add flour and stir well to coat chicken. Add mushrooms, Dijon mustard, crème fraîche and chicken stock. Stir well.

Add thyme, rosemary and nutmeg. Season with salt and pepper. Bring to a slow simmer, stirring frequently. Remove from the heat and set aside.

Using 1 sheet of pastry, carefully line a 20 cm pie dish.

Blind bake for 10 minutes, remove baking beads and bake a further 5 minutes. (If using a perforated pie dish, there is no need to blind bake)

Remove and discard thyme and rosemary sprigs from pan. Carefully spoon the slightly cooled chicken mixture into the pie case. Cover with remaining pastry sheet.

Mix egg and milk together to make an egg wash. Brush over pastry top and bake for 30 minutes until golden.

Allow to stand for 5-10 minutes before serving.

https://youtu.be/aozC4aJtOsc

Gluten free chicken parma

Serves 2

You would be hard pressed to find a pub in Australia that doesn't have a "chicken parma" on the menu. Chicken Parmigiana is a meal adapted from the traditional melanzane alla parmigiana which is breaded aubergine (eggplant) served with tomato and cheese topping.

Chicken parma is a quick meal that is easily cooked up fresh after work for dinner. Often served with chips and salad, it makes a meal that suits everyone in the family.

For a gluten-free version, I tried many different forms of GF breadcrumbs, commercially bought, and homemade. None gave the crunch that panko crumbs provide. There are some gluten-free panko crumbs available, but they are not easily sourced. It wasn't until I tried polenta as the crumb coating that I found the perfect substitute.

Polenta is a cornmeal. Often it is mixed with water, butter, and cheese and served as an accompaniment to stews, or allowed to go firm and fried. In this case, however, we use the polenta dry. It forms a crisp coating that keeps the chicken fillet moist inside. There are no restrictions on the flavours you can add to the polenta crust. I generally use dried mixed herbs but also add chilli or grated parmesan to make a more interesting crust.

The tomato base is an important ingredient in this recipe. I use my homemade tomato sauce as it has a depth of flavour with the spices added during the cooking. Alternatively, you can use a commercially bought passata or sugo. Tomato paste is too intense in flavour and acidity to use in this case.

The addition of ham on top of the tomato base is one filled with controversy. Many pubs leave this out. The choice is yours.

The cheese needs to be one that melts and browns well. Parmesan is often used. I prefer Jarlsberg cheese because it browns well and has a low salt content. Again use a cheese that suits your family preferences.

- ½ cup polenta
- 1 tbl dried mixed herbs
- 3 slices Jarlsberg cheese
- 3 tbl tomato sugo
- 2 chicken breasts
- 2 slices ham
- 1 egg

Preheat oven to 180°C fan/200°C.

Using a meat mallet, flatten out the chicken breasts to ensure evenness of cooking.

Lightly beat egg in a medium-sized bowl.

Combine polenta and herbs together. Place on a plate.

To prepare the schnitzel, dip chicken breast in egg until well covered. Place breast onto the plate with polenta. Coat both sides, pressing down on the polenta to ensure it is stuck well.

In a hot frypan, add a splash of olive oil. Gently fry each schnitzel for 2-3 minutes on each side until the crust is lightly golden. Place schnitzel on an oven tray. Spread each schnitzel with half the tomato sauce. Place a slice of ham on each fillet. Add a slice and a half of cheese to the top.

Bake in the oven for approximately 20 minutes.

https://youtu.be/2y1uXmpnwR0

Crumbed mussels

Makes 30

It is amazing how many myths there are around the humble sea creature, the mussel. They are such a versatile food that can be served in so many ways, low in fat, high in essential minerals. Luckily for me, they are farmed in Corio Bay, just an hour's drive from home - so freshness is guaranteed.

I am privileged to have had the opportunity over the last nine years to volunteer at the Portarlington Mussel Festival, with the last seven conducting cooking demonstrations. I have had the opportunity to get to know one of the farmers, Jenny from Mr Mussel, and she has taught me a lot about these amazing creatures.

The Blue Mussels are farmed on ropes suspended metres above the seabed. The female mussels are orange, and the males are a white/cream colour.

Fresh mussels can be stored in the fridge for 7-10 days. Keep the mussels covered with a damp tea-towel that you change every 2-3 days.

When preparing mussels, allow them to rinse in a sink of cool water for about 10 minutes. This allows them to open and release some of the seawater and grit. Discard any with a broken shell or that are open and do not close when tapped on the bench. The mussels are then ready to prepare.

De-bearding a mussel. There is a hard way and an easy way. The hard way - holding the mussel with the pointy end pointing to the sky, take hold of the beard, and sharply pull it downwards. Then add the mussel to your prepared sauce. The easy way - steam the mussels open in an empty pan over medium heat (3-5 minutes). The beards can then be easily removed with a gentle tug. Any juices left in the pan can be strained through a fine mesh strainer and kept in the freezer. This mussel stock is perfect in risottos or paella.

Many people believe that any mussels that do not open during cooking need to be thrown out and not eaten. This is TOTALLY INCORRECT. All the mussels in the pan are dead - you've just cooked them! When opening these mussels using the point of a sharp knife, be wary, as the shell will often contain hot water that can scald you.

- 1 kg mussels
- 2 beaten eggs
- 1 cup plain flour (GF)
- 1½ cups freshly made bread crumbs (GF)
- Good-sized pinch of pimento
- Salt and pepper to taste
- Rice bran oil for deep frying

Steam the mussels open in a pan covered with a tight-fitting lid. As they open, remove them to a bowl.

Combine flour, salt, pepper and pimento in a bowl.

De-beard mussels, and remove mussels from shell, keeping half of each shell for serving.

Coat mussels with flour, followed by egg and finally breadcrumbs.

Heat oil in a deep pan or wok (180°C). Oil should be kept between 160°C-190°C for perfect results.

Deep fry crumbed mussels in small batches until golden. Be careful not to overheat oil as this will lead to mussels becoming overcooked and tough.

To serve, place back into half shells and serve with mayonnaise.

Notes:

1. When steaming the mussels, don' be tempted to overcrowd the pan. A kilo of mussels is usually 2-3 batches depending on the size of your pan.

2. As the mussels are damp when removed from the shell, make sure that you coat them well in the flour and breadcrumbs to reduce the risk of the oil spitting, and to ensure that the mussel stays moist inside the crispy crumb coating.

Pumpkin, spinach and feta frittata

Serves 6

This is one of my most versatile recipes. It's perfect for picnics, lunch with girlfriends, a light dinner, anytime really. The variations are limitless. I often add crispy bacon or sun-dried tomatoes - whatever you have on hand. The frittata is perfect served hot, at room temperature, or cold.

A frittata is an egg-based dish, a little like a crust-less quiche, which makes it perfect to serve for those who need a gluten-free meal, without having to make any adjustments to the recipe.

- 650 g pumpkin, roughly chopped
- 300 g potato, coarsely chopped
- 125 g spinach
- 200 g feta cheese
- 100 g grated tasty cheese
- 8 eggs
- 1 small red onion, thinly sliced

Preheat oven to 200°C fan/220°C.

Grease a large baking tin.

Cook pumpkin in a microwave on high for 5 minutes until just tender. Cook potato in the same way for 4 minutes. Combine potato and pumpkin in a large bowl and allow to cool.

Using a fork, crumble feta cheese. Lightly beat eggs.

Add feta, tasty cheese, spinach and eggs to the pumpkin and potato. Stir gently to combine.

Transfer mixture to the baking tin. Top with red onion.

Bake for 20-25 minutes, or until firm. Allow to sit in the tin for 5 minutes before serving.

https://youtu.be/JFqGYT-5wSU

Gluten free sourdough bread

Makes 1 loaf

The quality of commercially available bread is one of the hardest things to accept after a coeliac diagnosis. Supermarket loaves are often small, frozen and thawed — meaning they can't be refrozen — while $12 specialty loaves from emerging gluten-free bakeries can be hit or miss. All you really want is a slice of bread that works in a sandwich or holds together when toasted for breakfast.

For a long time, even that modest goal felt out of reach. But after plenty of trial and error — and yes, a few tears — I finally found a homemade loaf that delivers.

Sourdough bread takes time, but it's not technically difficult. It just needs patience to prove. There are three stages: sourdough starter, sponge, and dough. The starter takes five days to develop, but with some care, it'll last for years. You can use flours like quinoa, sorghum, buckwheat, or millet as a base. I prefer brown rice flour — it's easy to find and gives a mild flavour.

This recipe is adapted from English chef Naomi Devlin. While she adds yeast to the sponge, I don't think it's necessary — the bread rises beautifully without it.

Sourdough Starter

Day 1:

- 150 g brown rice flour
- 200 g tepid filtered water

Mix together, and cover with a plate. Leave in a warm place for 24 hours.

Day 2:

- 45 g brown rice flour
- 60 g tepid filtered water

Stir the mixture. Add the flour and water, and stir again. Re-cover and leave for another 24 hours.

Day 3:

- 45 g brown rice flour
- 60 g tepid filtered water

Stir the mixture. Add the flour and water, and stir again. The mixture should be starting to bubble and smell a bit yeasty. Re-cover and leave for another 24 hours.

Day 4:

- 90 g brown rice flour
- 120 g tepid filtered water

Stir the mixture. Add the flour and water, and stir again. Re-cover and leave for another 24 hours.

Your starter can now be stored in a plastic container in the fridge. However, it does need to be fed at least every two weeks by bringing it up to room temperature and adding 90g brown rice flour and 120g tepid filtered water.

On the day you're making bread, add 75g rice flour and 100g warm water to the starter at least an hour before making the sponge.

Sponge:
- 200 g sourdough starter
- 125 g rice flour
- 25 g buckwheat flour
- 25 g sorghum flour
- 300 ml tepid water

Sourdough:
- 100 g potato flour
- 100 g tapioca flour
- 25 g maize flour
- 25 g ground linseed, plus extra for tin
- 25 g salted butter
- 1 large egg
- 15 g muscovado sugar (or dark brown sugar)
- 7 g fine sea salt
- 1 tsp apple cider vinegar
- 25 g pepitas seeds (optional)
- 50 g pine nuts (optional)

To make the sponge:

Mix all the sponge ingredients together in a bowl, cover and leave in a warm place for 2-4 hours, or in a cool place overnight.

To make the dough:

In a large bowl combine the prepared sponge with all remaining ingredients except pepitas seeds. Mix to combine.

Prepare your loaf tin by greasing well with butter and coating with the extra linseed.

Pour the dough into the tin and tap to level the dough. Sprinkle with pepitas seeds. Set aside in a warm place for 60 - 90 minutes, until the dough has risen by ⅓ and small cracks appear on the surface. Be very gentle with the dough, as a sharp knock to the tin can cause the loaf to collapse.

Preheat oven to 210°C fan/230°C. Place an empty tin in the bottom of the oven to heat up.

Carefully place the loaf into the oven. For the perfect crust sprinkle the top with a bit of cold water. Pour boiling water into the hot, empty tin to generate steam. Bake for 15 minutes, then reduce the oven temperature to 180°C fan/ 200°C and bake for a further 45 minutes. Allow the bread to cool in the tin.

Resist the temptation to slice the loaf until it has cooled completely.

https://youtu.be/e3OHvHdSNNU

Gluten free spiced fruit sourdough

Makes 1 loaf

The scent of toasted raisin toast wafting through the house evokes strong memories from my childhood – a rare treat indeed.

In the thriving cafe culture of my hometown, Melbourne, Australia, artisan fruit breads are commonplace on cafe breakfast menus. These breads always contain large pieces of various dried fruits and are thickly cut. They are often served with cultured butter and chunky, homemade jams or marmalade. They always look mouth-watering, and I must admit to pangs of jealousy when Myles orders them.

As any coeliac knows, finding good gluten-free bread products can be challenging, especially when it comes to specialty breads. So, for the past six months or so, I've been experimenting with turning my gluten-free sourdough into a mouth-watering spiced fruit sourdough loaf. I've found that I achieve a better loaf if I pour off any hooch (the liquid that collects on top of your starter) before I make the sourdough sponge. Hooch is the alcohol produced as the wild yeast in your starter ferments. It's a sign that your starter is hungry. The more frequently you feed the starter, the less hooch is produced, leading to a better rise in your dough but a less sour flavour. It's all a balancing act.

There's no right or wrong selection of dried fruits; it's all based on what you have in the pantry and your family's preferences. In this recipe, I've used dried apricots, dried figs and sultanas. Sometimes, I add dried cranberries or blueberries for a change. The addition of xanthan gum is necessary when adding the dried fruit to ensure the fruit bread maintains its shape despite the additional weight of the fruit.

Proving the dough is an inexact science unless you have a proving cabinet that can regulate the temperature and humidity to yield perfect results every time. It's important not to leave the dough to prove for more than 90 minutes, or it will dry out. Even if it hasn't risen to the top of the tin, bake it when you reach the 90-minute mark. It will continue to rise in the oven.

The basis of this recipe is my sourdough bread.

- 1 basic sourdough mixture
- 30 g dried apricots
- 70 g dried figs
- 100 g dried sultanas
- 2 tsp mixed spice
- 1 tsp ground cinnamon
- ¼ tsp ground cloves
- 1 tsp xanthan gum
- 1 tsp freshly ground nutmeg

Day 1

Prepare sourdough sponge as per standard recipe. Let flavours develop overnight.

Day 2

Follow standard recipe up to putting dough into the prepared bread tin.

Cut the apricots and figs into thirds.

Add all dried fruit and spices to the dough and mix well.

Grease the tin well with butter. Pour in the dough and smooth out the top.

Place in a warm spot to prove until risen to the top of the tin (maximum 90 minutes).

Preheat oven to 210°C fan/230°C. Place an empty tin in the bottom of the oven to heat up.

Gently place the loaf into the oven. Sprinkle the top of the loaf with cold water to create a superb crust. Pour boiling water into the hot empty tin to generate steam. Bake for 15 minutes, then reduce the oven temperature to 180°C and continue to bake for another 45 minutes. Allow the loaf to cool in the tin. Resist the temptation to slice the loaf until it has completely cooled.

https://youtu.be/e_yYkZ9WpyY

Zucchini slice

Serves 4-6

Anyone with a home veggie patch understands the challenges of managing an abundant harvest. Summer is a season where that one overlooked zucchini (courgette) can suddenly balloon to over a kilo before you realise it. This usually happens just when your fridge is already filled with sweet, young zucchinis. This classic recipe is perfect for both: the more tougher, older zucchinis as well as the tender young ones.

Ideal when served warm with a crisp salad, this zucchini slice is also a hit in school lunchboxes, perfect for picnics, and it freezes well to boot.

Growing up, I never had zucchini slice. However, the first meal that Myles' mum cooked for me was a version of this dish.

This basic recipe also allows for various tweaks and additions. Consider incorporating some finely diced chorizo, grated carrot, diced tomatoes, crumbled feta, or thinly sliced red onion on top before baking—the possibilities are endless.

For best results, cook the slice in either a slice tin (16 x 26 cm) or a Lamington pan (20 x 30 cm). These rectangular pans with shallow sides (around 3 cm high) are ideal.

- 5 eggs
- 375 g zucchini, grated (approx. 2 medium)
- 150 g self-raising flour (GF optional)
- 1 tsp baking powder (omit if not using GF flour)
- 1 large onion, finely chopped
- 200 g bacon, rind removed and finely chopped (approx. 3 rashers)
- 1 cup grated tasty cheese
- 60 ml vegetable oil

Preheat oven to 160°C fan/180°C.

In a large bowl, beat the eggs well. Add the flour and beat until smooth. Add the zucchini, onion, bacon, cheese, and oil and stir until well combined.

Grease a Lamington pan and line with baking paper, making sure the paper hangs over all sides. Pour the mixture into the pan and bake for 30-40 minutes until the top is brown.

Allow to cool in the tin for 5 minutes before gently lifting out onto a board. Cut into squares and serve with a crisp salad.

https://youtu.be/HqWN1EYhpj4

Beth's pumpkin, spinach & prosciutto salad

Serves 4-6

I am blessed to have a number of friends who are amazing cooks and always happy to share recipes and tips. One of these is the amazing Beth. Beth makes cooking for a crowd always seem so easy – she whips up interesting salads, marinades, and delicious desserts, all of which seem to appear out of her TARDIS-like fridge.

This salad is one of Beth's. Easily scaled up or down to suit the size of the crowd, it can be prepped the day before and quickly assembled as required. It's flexible too – I've added toasted pine nuts, or swapped out the parmesan for crumbled feta just for a change. But you always come back to the classic recipe – a real winner!

Thanks, Beth, for sharing this recipe and allowing me to share it with the world.

- 1 kg pumpkin, peeled and cubed
- 100 g baby spinach
- 50 g shaved parmesan
- 100 g prosciutto
- Olive oil
- Balsamic vinegar

Preheat the oven to 190°C fan/210°C.

Place cubed pumpkin in a single layer on an oiled baking tray. Separate the prosciutto and lay it across the pumpkin.

Roast for 20 minutes. Remove the prosciutto and, using a spatula, turn the pumpkin gently. Continue roasting the pumpkin until tender, approximately 10 minutes.

Remove from the oven and, while still warm, loosen the pumpkin from the tray. Allow to cool.

Break up the prosciutto and set it aside.

Place baby spinach onto a serving platter and drizzle with 1 tbl of balsamic vinegar. Arrange the cooled pumpkin on top and sprinkle with parmesan. Drizzle with more balsamic vinegar.

To finish, sprinkle with prosciutto.

Additions: Crumbled feta instead of parmesan, toasted pine nuts.

Lamb shanks and cheesy polenta

Serves 2

Perfect on a winter's night, this is definitely comfort food! The rich, slow-cooked flavour of the lamb is perfectly paired with creamy, cheesy polenta.

Polenta is cornmeal. Traditionally, polenta was made from a variety of grains and was extensively eaten in Northern and Central Italy. Today, polenta comes in two varieties: traditional and instant. The process for cooking is exactly the same; however, the cooking time is very different. Traditional polenta takes about 30 minutes, whereas instant takes about 10 minutes.

- 2 lamb shanks
- Olive oil
- 400 g crushed tomatoes
- 1 brown onion, chopped finely
- 2 cloves garlic, sliced thinly
- 1 red chilli, sliced finely
- 150 g kalamata olives
- 50 g capers
- 1 cup puy lentils
- 1 cup red wine
- 1 cup water

Cheesy polenta
- ½ cup polenta
- 2 cups water
- Salt
- 150 g pecorino cheese, grated
- Knob of butter

Preheat oven to 180°C fan/200°C.

Using a heavy-based casserole dish that is also ovenproof, heat oil. Seal the lamb shanks all over, then remove from the pan. Gently fry onion, garlic and chilli until soft. Deglaze the pan with the red wine.

Return the lamb shanks to the pan, add all remaining ingredients, and stir.

Place in the oven and cook for 90 minutes. Serve with cheesy polenta.

Polenta:

Bring salted water to the boil.

Gradually add the polenta in a thin steady stream, stirring constantly until all the polenta is incorporated into the water. Don't add the polenta too quickly or it will turn lumpy. Continue to stir on a low heat until the polenta comes away from the sides of the pot. Add butter and stir until incorporated.

Add cheese and stir.

https://youtu.be/9_biPVW-nJU

Corn fritters with roasted balsamic tomatoes

Serves 2

To understand the choice for vegetarian or vegan lifestyles, I've delved into the environmental and ethical impacts of meat consumption. Michael Pollan's book, "The Omnivore's Dilemma," urges us to consider how modern lifestyles have affected the planet and animal welfare. It highlights our disconnection from food origins and traditions. This resonates with the Slow Food movement, which champions local food cultures while countering our dwindling connection to what we eat. I recommend Pollan's book for a deeper understanding of these issues.

Back to today's recipe, which, in a small way, contributes to change by using fresh, locally-sourced ingredients. A quick Google search for corn fritter recipes yields thousands of hits. This recipe is easy to scale up to feed a crowd, tasty, and reheats well the next day. It's also simple to make and looks like something you'd get in a café, without needing any fancy equipment.

I prefer to use fresh corn when it's in season. To prepare it, remove the husk and silk, break off the stem, and place this end on a board. Holding the cob at the pointy end, use a sharp knife to cut downwards in a gentle sawing motion. Don't cut too close to the cob's centre, as it's not only hard to cut but also results in "woody" ends mixed in with the kernels. If fresh corn isn't available, frozen corn is the next best option. Frozen vegetables are usually snap-frozen within hours of being picked, so when thawed, they're quite close to fresh in taste and texture. The kernels take only 10-15 minutes to thaw before you can use them. Canned corn is another option but has been cooked during the canning process. Make sure to drain it well, as canned corn will make your batter wetter, requiring a bit of extra flour for adjustment.

There are many tweaks you can make to this recipe. I like to add a pinch of cayenne pepper to the flour for a bit of heat. Other serving suggestions include: pairing with sour cream and some pickled jalapeño slices, or with a poached egg (and some crispy bacon for the non-vegetarians).

- 300 g corn kernels (approx. 2 cobs)
- ½ small red onion, chopped
- 1 egg
- 1 tbl coriander leaves (including some stems)
- ½ tsp sea salt
- ½ cup plain flour (GF)
- ½ tsp baking powder
- 2 tbl olive oil
- Freshly ground black pepper

- 250 g truss cherry tomatoes
- 1 tbl balsamic vinegar
- 2 tbl olive oil

Serve with sliced avocado and lime wedges.

Preheat oven to 180°C fan/200°C.

Place cherry tomatoes in a shallow dish. Combine vinegar and oil and brush onto tomatoes. Bake for 10-15 minutes until soft.

Put aside 125 g of corn kernels. In a food processor, place the remainder of the corn, coriander, onion, egg, salt and pepper. Blend until mostly pureed - leave a few lumps. Transfer to a bowl and stir through remaining corn, flour and baking powder until just combined.

In a heavy based frypan, heat olive oil on a medium heat. Using a large spoon, drop mixture into the frypan and cook on each side until golden (1.5-2 minutes each side).

Serve with tomatoes, avocado wedges and a twist of lime.

https://youtu.be/BQ0fB5jGWHo

Index

A
- almond
  - Almond biscuits (Nonna biscuits) 8
- ANZAC biscuits 190
- apple
  - Apple and rhubarb crumble 192
  - Apple and rhubarb tart 194
  - Gluten free apple pie with flakey pastry 104
  - Tarte Tatin (French apple tart) 70
- arancini
  - Mushroom arancini with goats cheese 170
- asparagus
  - Asparagus with speck and gorgonzola 218
  - Gluten free asparagus and ricotta quiche 100

B
- banana
  - Gluten free banana bread 106
- beef
  - Beef burgundy 76
  - Bragioli (Beef olives) 158
  - Lasagne 166
  - Massaman curry 146
  - Prosciutto wrapped beef with mushrooms 176
- biscuits
  - Almond biscuits (Nonna biscuits) 8
  - Dark chocolate florentines 152
  - Gluten free ANZAC biscuits 190
  - Gluten free kingston biscuits 198
- blackberry(s)
  - Rustic berry tart 66
- blueberry(s)
  - Blueberry buttermilk pancakes 108
  - Rustic berry tart 66
- Bragioli (Beef olives) 158
- bread
  - Gluten free banana bread 106
  - Gluten free sourdough bread 230
  - Gluten free spiced fruit sourdough 234
- brownie
  - Chocolate brownies 110

C
- cake
  - Chocolate lava cake 112
  - Christmas cake 12
  - Gluten free lemon and poppyseed muffins 202
  - Gluten free lime and coconut friands 204
  - Gluten free red velvet cupcakes 116
  - Raspberry pistachio friands 210
  - Sponge cake with passionfruit icing 214
- Cannelé 46
- casserole
  - Chicken cacciatore 160
  - French styled chicken casserole 92
  - Lamb shanks and cheesy polenta 240
- Celeriac and potato dauphinoise 88
- cheese
  - Gluten free pumpkin soup & cheesy damper 36
  - Ham and cheese potato croquettes 80
- cheesecake
  - Basque cheesecake 44
  - Cherry cheesecake 48
- cherry
  - Cherry cheesecake 48
  - Roast duck with cherry sauce 90
- chicken
  - Black pepper chicken 126
  - Chicken and mushroom pie 222
  - Chicken basil stir fry 128
  - Chicken cacciatore 160
  - Chicken enchiladas 120
  - Chicken tagine and jewelled rice 162
  - French styled chicken casserole 92
  - Gluten free chicken parma 224
  - Pomegranate chicken 142
- chocolate
  - Chocolate brownies 110
  - Chocolate lava cake 112
  - Chocolate raspberry mousse 50
  - Dark chocolate florentines 152
  - Dark chocolate rocky road 216
  - Double choc raspberry muffins 20
  - Gluten free chocolate self saucing puddings 10
  - Gluten free red velvet cupcakes 116
  - Raspberry macarons with dark chocolate ganache 72
- chorizo
  - Mussels with tomato and chorizo 84
- Christmas
  - Christmas cake 12
  - Christmas mince pies 16
  - Dark chocolate florentines 152
  - Gluten free Christmas pudding 18
  - Traditional shortbread 68
- coconut
  - Chilli and coconut prawns 144
  - Coconut macaroons 52
  - Gluten free lime and coconut friands 204
  - Raspberry coconut slice 208
- Corn fritters with roasted balsamic tomatoes 242
- Cornish pasties 78
- Crema Catalana 54
- Crème caramel 74
- crêpes
  - Gluten free crêpes 56
- croquettes
  - Ham and cheese potato croquettes 80
- crumble

Apple and rhubarb crumble 192
cupcake
   Gluten free red velvet cupcakes 116
custard
   Crema Catalana 54
   Crème caramel 74
   Panna cotta with roasted peaches 156

damper
   Gluten free pumpkin soup
   & cheesy damper 36
date
   Sticky date pudding 28
dessert
   Apple and rhubarb crumble 192
   Apple and rhubarb tart 194
   Baked pears 42
   Cannelé 46
   Chocolate raspberry mousse 50
   Gluten free chocolate self saucing puddings 10
   Lemon delicious pudding 200
   Lemon tart 60
   Panna cotta with roasted peaches 156
   Pavlova 206
   Rustic berry tart 66
   Sticky date pudding 28
   Tarte Tatin (French apple tart) 70
   Tropical tiramisu 30
donuts
   Italian ricotta donuts
   (Frittelle Di Ricotta) 154
duck
   Roast duck with cherry sauce 90

eggs
   Shakshuka (Baked eggs) 172
enchiladas
   Chicken enchiladas 120

falafels
   Falafels with tahini sauce 148
Fettuccine carbonara 182
fish
   Crispy yuan salmon 130
   Fish pie 96
florentines
   Dark chocolate florentines 152
friand
   Gluten free lime and coconut friands 204
   Raspberry pistachio friands 210
frittata
   Pumpkin, spinach and feta frittata 228

gingerbread
   Gluten free gingerbread 58
Gnocchi with burnt butter, sage, and gorgonzola 168
Goat curry 134

ham
   Baked ham with maple syrup & mustard glaze 32
   Ham and cheese potato croquettes 80
   Pea and ham soup 34
hot cross buns
   Gluten free hot cross buns 22
   Gluten-free hot cross buns (Version 2) 24

J
Jelly slice 196

K
Kartoffelsalat (potato salad) 98
Kingston biscuits 198

L
lamb
   Lamb shanks and cheesy polenta 240
   Moroccan lamb kefta tagine 174
Lasagne 166
lemon
   Gluten free lemon and poppyseed muffins 202
   Lemon delicious pudding 200
   Lemon tart 60
lime
   Gluten free lime and coconut friands 204

M
macarons
   Raspberry macarons with dark chocolate
   ganache 72
macaroons
   Coconut macaroons 52
madeleines
   Gluten free madeleines 62
Massaman curry 146
mince pies
   Christmas mince pies 16
mousse
   Chocolate raspberry mousse 50
muffins
   Double choc raspberry muffins 20
   Gluten free lemon and poppyseed muffins 202
mushroom(s)
   Chicken and mushroom pie 222
   Mushroom arancini with goats cheese 170
   Prosciutto wrapped beef with mushrooms 176
mussels
   Crumbed mussels 226
   Curried mussels (Goan style) 132
   Mussels with tomato and chorizo 84
   Tempura mussels 140

O
octopus
   Pulpo con pimentón
   (Spanish octopus with paprika) 94
Okonomiyaki 136

P
paella
   Traditional seafood paella (Paella de marisco) 82
pancakes
   Blueberry buttermilk pancakes 108
   Gluten free pancakes & strawberries 114
   Okonomiyaki 136

panna cotta
    Panna cotta with roasted peaches 156
pasta
    Gnocchi with burnt butter, sage, and gorgonzola 168
    Home made fettuccine carbonara 182
    Imqarrun il-forn (Maltese baked pasta) 164
    Lasagne 166
    Ravioli 184
pasties
    Cornish pasties 78
Pavlova 206
pea(s)
    Pea and ham soup 34
pear
    Baked pears 42
pie
    Chicken and mushroom pie 222
    Fish pie 96
    Gluten free apple pie with flakey pastry 104
Pizza 180
pomegranate
    Pomegranate chicken 142
Porchetta 178
pork
    Porchetta 178
Potato rösti 86
potato(s)
    Celeriac and potato dauphinoise 88
    Ham and cheese potato croquettes 80
    Kartoffelsalat (potato salad) 98
    Potato rösti 86
prawns
    Chilli and coconut prawns 144
    Traditional seafood paella (Paella de marisco) 82
profiteroles
    Gluten free profiteroles 64
prosciutto
    Prosciutto wrapped beef with mushrooms 176
pudding
    Gluten free chocolate self saucing puddings 10
    Gluten free Christmas pudding 18
    Lemon delicious pudding 200
    Sticky date pudding 28
    Yorkshire pudding 38
pumpkin
    Gluten free pumpkin soup & cheesy damper 36
    Pumpkin, spinach and feta frittata 228

Q

quesadilla
    Gluten free quesadilla 122
quiche
    Gluten free asparagus and ricotta quiche 100

R

raspberry(s)
    Chocolate raspberry mousse 50
    Double choc raspberry muffins 20
    Raspberry coconut slice 208
    Raspberry macarons with dark chocolate ganache 72
    Raspberry pistachio friands 210
    Rustic berry tart 66
Ravioli 184
Rice paper rolls 138

S

salad
    Beth's pumpkin, spinach & prosciutto salad 238
    Kartoffelsalat (potato salad) 98
    Quinoa tabouli 186
salmon
    Crispy yuan salmon 130
Sausage rolls 220
Scones 212
seafood
    Chilli and coconut prawns 144
    Crispy yuan salmon 130
    Crumbed mussels 226
    Curried mussels (Goan style) 132
    Fish pie 96
    Mussels with tomato and chorizo 84
    Tempura mussels 140
    Traditional seafood paella (Paella de marisco) 82
Shakshuka (Baked eggs) 172
shortbread
    Traditional shortbread 68
slices
    Jelly slice 196
    Raspberry coconut slice 208
soup
    Gluten free pumpkin soup & cheesy damper 36
    Pea and ham soup 34
sourdough
    Gluten free sourdough bread 230
    Gluten free spiced fruit sourdough 234
strawberry(s)
    Gluten free pancakes & strawberries 114
    Rustic berry tart 66

T

Tabouli 186
tagine
    Chicken tagine and jewelled rice 162
    Moroccan lamb kefta tagine 174
tart
    Apple and rhubarb tart 194
    Lemon tart 60
    Rustic berry tart 66
    Tarte Tatin (French apple tart) 70
Tarte Tatin (French apple tart) 70
tempura
    Tempura mussels 140
tiramisu
    Tropical tiramisu 30
tomato
    Mussels with tomato and chorizo 84

W

waffles
    Gluten free waffles 118

Yorkshire pudding 38

Zucchini slice 236

Journeys Never Really End

As this chapter of Rie's Kitchen draws to a close, I'm reminded that journeys never really end — they just pause, pivot, or evolve. This book is rooted in my own story — my travels, my diagnosis, my family — but I hope it has also helped you discover something new in your own kitchen.

Every recipe here is a kind of souvenir. A moment, a place, a person. These dishes have been shaped by market mornings in France, cooking classes in Morocco, conversations at the kitchen table, and years of filming in our little Melbourne kitchen. Whether you've made them as written or given them your own spin, I hope they've become part of your story too.

Cooking, like travelling, teaches us curiosity, patience, and joy. It opens doors to other cultures and unexpected discoveries — and somehow brings us closer to home at the same time. The heart of each dish is the same: to nourish, to share, to celebrate.

Every family has its own rituals. A special spoon for stirring. A "secret" ingredient. A story that gets told every time a certain dish is made. Now that you've spent time with mine, I'd love to think you're beginning new rituals of your own.

Thank you for letting me be part of your table — for trying the recipes, sharing your feedback, and making space in your own journey for mine. Let's keep cooking, keep sharing, and keep finding magic in the everyday.

The best meals are yet to come.

Ciao, Rie.

Rue de l'Horloge, Dinan, France — a moment on this journey